The Poetry of Jonathan Swift

Allusion and the Development of a Poetic Style

The Poetry of Jonathan Swift

Allusion and the Development of a Poetic Style

PETER J. SCHAKEL

THE UNIVERSITY OF WISCONSIN PRESS

Published 1978

The University of Wisconsin Press
Box 1379, Madison, Wisconsin 53701

The University of Wisconsin Press, Ltd.
1 Gower St., London WC1E 6HA, England

First printing
Printed in the United States of America

For LC CIP information see the colophon

ISBN 0-299-07650-4

Publication of this book has been made possible in part
by a grant from the Andrew W. Mellon Foundation

To Karen

Contents

Acknowledgments

Research for this study was aided by two grants from the American Philosophical Society—one from the Penrose Fund and one from the Johnson Fund, by fellowships from the William Andrews Clark Memorial Library in Los Angeles and the Newberry Library in Chicago, and by three grants from Hope College—the Julia Van Raalte Reimold Faculty Study Award, a grant from the Matthew J. and Anne C. Wilson Foundation Faculty Development Program, and an award from a Mellon Faculty Development Grant. I am deeply grateful for the encouragement and support these grants have provided.

I am grateful also to the editors and publishers of several journals for permission to reprint materials from the following articles: "Swift's 'Verses Wrote in a Lady's Ivory Table-Book,' " *The Explicator* [Heldref Publications], May, 1970, Item 83; "Virgil and the Dean: Christian and Classical Allusion in 'The Legion Club,' " *Studies in Philology* [The University of North Carolina Press], 70 (October 1973), 427–38; "The Politics of Opposition in 'Verses on the Death of Dr. Swift,' " *Modern Language*

Quarterly [The University of Washington], 35 (September 1974), 246–56; "Swift's 'dapper Clerk' and the Matrix of Allusions in 'Cadenus and Vanessa,' " *Criticism* [Wayne State University Press], 17 (Summer 1975), 246–61; and "Swift's Remedy for Love: The 'Scatological' Poems," *Papers on Language and Literature* [Southern Illinois University Press], 14 (Spring 1978), 137–47.

I am indebted to a number of persons who encouraged and assisted me during the research and writing. Several persons, at one point or another, read and commented on individual chapters or portions of chapters: Leland Ryken, Maximillian Novak, Felicity Nussbaum, Paula Backscheider, and David M. Vieth. Irvin Ehrenpreis provided good counsel on several occasions. James R. Wilson, who stimulated my interest in Swift in an undergraduate course at Central College, read the entire manuscript, as did Timothy Keegan and my colleague Charles A. Huttar—each pointed out problems and errors and offered valuable suggestions for improvements. Finally, I am grateful to my wife, Karen, for such tangible help as reading and commenting on chapters in progress, typing early drafts of several chapters, and checking proofs, and for the intangible but invaluable supports of confidence, patience, understanding, and encouragement throughout the project.

The Poetry of Jonathan Swift

Allusion and the Development of a Poetic Style

Introduction

Lord Bathurst, writing to Jonathan Swift, warns him to answer his letter, or "I'll take your works to Peices & show you that it is all borrow'd or stoln . . . have not you borrow'd thoughts from Virgil & Horace, at least I am sure I have seen something like them in those Books."[1] Bathurst was referring to Swift's prose works, many of whose allusions have been identified by critics and proved valuable to understanding Swift's techniques and intentions. But surprisingly, the borrowings in his verse have not been examined to any significant extent, even where Swift acknowledged indebtedness himself. If an understanding of his poetry comparable to that of his prose is to be attained, it must begin with his allusions. In his major poems, Swift often used allusions to introduce a set of conventions or a structural framework, to clarify or reinforce his themes, and to establish or strengthen his tones. This book is an effort to supply a basic and necessary study of Swift's poetic art from which further exploration can proceed and without which very fundamental aspects of his art and meaning will inevitably be overlooked.

Attention to allusions is important for understanding not only the structure of Swift's verse but also its substance, Truth. To say that Swift sought "realism" in his poetry has become something of a commonplace. A more accurate assessment is that his central concern was truth. He sought to write, according to words that either he or Pope added to one of his poems, "Something in Verse as true as Prose."[2] The words *truth, truly,* and *true* occur at least 170 times in his poems and are a recurring motif characterizing and unifying them. In a key passage on the value, or even purpose, of poetry, Swift asserts that "Truth shines the brighter, clad in Verse."[3] Not only is truth to be as much a concern of poetry as of prose, but its clarity and impact are increased by the sounds and patterns of poetry. Swift's search for truth in verse is revealed to a large extent through allusions, as he raised or reinforced central thoughts by alluding to the works of others, incorporating his ideas with those of others to gain breadth, complexity, and universality.

An approach to Swift's allusions must not be patterned on the methods critics have developed for the poems of Alexander Pope, if indeed Pope actually intended, as Earl R. Wasserman maintained, to invite each reader "to exercise . . . his own invention by contemplating the relevances of the entire allusive context and its received interpretation."[4] Swift's poems, at any rate, do not rely for their vitality on "a set of complexly acting and interacting attitudes which usually are so deeply and yet allusively incorporated that they can be overlooked by us, in our remoteness from his culture and its values."[5] Swift was rarely subtle about including allusions; usually, he footnoted them or even mentioned them within the poem itself. To a great extent, then, the important thing in a study of Swift's poetry is not the *discovery* of allusions, but the consideration of their *use* in the poems. I have focused therefore on explicit or repeated allusions, not on references to classical figures or quotations from literary works used in passing as decoration or as a means of expression. The emphasis of this study is on the way Swift, in his major poems, stays with allusions and develops structural and thematic supports for his verse through them.

Beyond their impact on technique and truth, allusions help assess Swift's growth as a poet. Swift's characteristic allusive method did not appear suddenly, fully developed, in his verse. That it required considerable experimentation and struggle is evident from a close inspection of the poems. Because those efforts are so apparent and because allusions, in their various manifestations, are at the heart of the poems, allusions offer a valuable index to Swift's development as a poet. From the early odes, where allusions from diverse sources sometimes decorate and sometimes deepen the style, to the early verse satires, often modeled after but not incorporating classical sources, to the later poems, strengthened by a union of structure and theme from external sources, steadily increasing control of and dependence upon allusion epitomize Swift's growth and maturation as a poet.

Allusions are also useful for considering Swift's own presence in the poems. It has long been recognized that Swift used fewer masks or disguises in his poems than his prose works: Swift is present in the poems in ways quite different from his presence in the prose. F. Elrington Ball wrote, several decades ago, "In his verse . . . he shows more clearly than in his prose his peculiar turn of thought, and he reveals his character in all its phases."[6] Critics, however, have generally not made that distinction or not taken advantage of it, despite Maurice Johnson's recent suggestion that Swift's personal involvement in his poems be given attention: "On reconsideration, I wonder whether the special quality in Swift's poems may not work through his own biographical presence. . . . As much as for any poet of his day, his own identity and his poetry seem inseparable."[7] This study, by its analyses of the poems, its attention to the choice of allusions, and its groupings of poems in chapters, endeavors to make Swift's presence a vital part of its consideration of the works.

Knowledge about the components of the poems or the growth

of the poet is finally less important than enjoyment of the works themselves. All of the poems discussed in this book except the early odes and "The Description of a Salamander" are humorous: some have humor as their main purpose; others use it in gaining broader ends. I have tried to keep that humor in view, often to highlight or clarify it, without spoiling it by overexplanation. Enjoyment of literature, of course, requires attention to texts, and the explications offered here are intended always to direct the reader to the poems themselves. Because many of Swift's poems are not well known, I have quoted from them liberally and included the entire texts of a few shorter poems. In sum, the goal of this book is to help readers toward a better understanding, a fuller appreciation, and a richer enjoyment of a poet who was, as Aubrey Williams recently asserted, "next to Pope . . . the best and most subtly allusive poet of his time."[8]

I

Cowley unto Himself
The Early Odes

It is perhaps not surprising that the Great Ode should have provided the model for Swift's earliest extant poetry. For an ambitious young writer, the ode was certainly a worthy aim, if not a very humble beginning. Swift's age regarded the ode as "one of the supreme expressions of poetry and itself as a supreme epoch in the history of the lyric, with its first master, Cowley, at least rivaling Pindar, [and] with Dryden secure among all competitors."[1] Despite the current popularity and influence of Dryden, however, Swift turned to the earlier writer, Abraham Cowley, for his main examples and inspiration. He acknowledged openly his admiration for and indebtedness to "rich Mr Cowly": "I find when I writt what pleases me I am Cowley to my self and can read it a hundred times over."[2] To be sure, few besides Swift have ever been pleased with his odes or reread them without compulsion. Stilted, banal, and even self-contradictory,[3] the odes are nevertheless of interest and importance in Swift's development as a poet. They show him trying, unsuccessfully, to

satisfy a need for fame and for order in life. They show him following an inclination to preach and, a bit later, to denounce.
And they show him attempting to find ways to control and
give structure to his thoughts, particularly through use of literary
allusions. A study of Swift's poetry must begin with the odes,
not so much for what they are as for their anticipations of and
influences upon what Swift was to become as an artist in both
prose and poetry.

I

The last of the odes, the "Ode to Dr. William Sancroft" (1692),
brings into sharpest focus a theme which runs through all of
them: the desire for order and stability. Influenced perhaps by
the uncertainties of his childhood or perhaps by the unsettled
religious and political conditions of his youth, Swift from the
first deplored "Men's Folly, Whimsyes, and Inconstancy."[4] Long
passages in the odes dwell on the unstableness of life:

> The herd beneath, who see the weathercock of state
>   Hung loosely on the Church's pinnacle,
> Believe it firm, because perhaps the day is mild and still;
> But when they find it turn with the first blast of fate,
>   By gazing upwards giddy grow,
>   And think the Church itself does so.
>   ("Ode to Sancroft," 73–78)[5]

And individual images and metaphors keep the theme of insta-
bility in the forefront almost constantly: images of that which
will "expire, / Consume, and perish," of a *Crowd of Atoms*
justling in a heap" or "the closing an unhappy Scene," of "weak
shapes wild and imperfect" passing or "images that sink in
streams," and of that which "crumbles . . . moulders . . . melts."[6]
The theme is communicated most powerfully, however, by
allusions—to Proteus, to the murmuring Jews wandering through
the wilderness, to Shakespeare's untended garden, to the Old

Testament flood.[7] The handling of allusions in these lines is typical:

> The crazy composition shews,
> Like that fantastic medley in the idol's toes,
> Made up of iron mixt with clay,
> This, crumbles into dust,
> That, moulders into rust,
> Or melts by the first show'r away.
> ("Ode to Sancroft," 137–42)

The allusion is to Nebuchadnezzar's dream of a great image with a head of gold, a body of silver and brass, legs of iron, and feet of iron mixed with clay. Daniel, in recalling the dream for the king, concludes: "Thou sawest till that a stone was cut out without hands, which smote the image upon his feet that were of iron and clay, and brake them to pieces" (Dan. 2:34). The vision accents the impermanence even of the great, seemingly unshakable kingdom of Babylon, whose eventual collapse the vision portends. Daniel's words of thanks to God for revealing the vision to him stress the theme of mutability and, at the same time, point to the only source and possessor of permanence: "Blessed be the name of God for ever and ever: for wisdom and might are his: And he changeth the times and the seasons: he removeth kings, and setteth up kings" (2:20–21). For the strength and stability of God, men have substituted the idol of Zeal, the turbulence and clamor of which are exposed and ridiculed by an allusion which also reinforces the broader theme of mutability.

Because of Swift's hunger for that which is firm, stable, secure, and reliable, he includes positive examples, both abstracted and embodied, in each ode. He looks to Virtue, Truth, and Goodness for stable, secure values and to the King, the Athenian Society, Sir William Temple, and Sancroft as worthy hero figures. His longing for permanence is strongly evidenced in the repeated used of "fixed": "But the Delight of *Doing Good* / Is fix't like Fate among the Stars."[8] The star image is also important; it recurs, for example, to depict Sancroft as a lasting exemplar of Truth and Virtue: "Nothing is fix'd that mortals see or know, / Unless, perhaps, some stars above be so" (143–44). Ten lines later Sancroft is addressed as "Kind Star" and is requested to show us "the way which leads to Christ" (161); the reference to Christ and the emphasis on a single route reinforce the sense of clarity and stability in the imagery. Peace, in the ode to Temple, is described as "forever green and flourishing" (85) and Truth, in the ode to Sancroft, is "eternal" (1),

> Nor does [its] essence fix'd depend on giddy circumstance
>   Of time or place,
> Two foolish guides in ev'ry sublunary dance.
>   (7–9)

The frequency with which similar themes, images, allusions, and illustrations occur in the odes suggests that they reflect Swift's personal ideas and feelings quite directly. Of course, all of Swift's works—the ironic as well as the nonironic ones—reveal his personality. Williams's statement that we are "closer to Swift in his verse . . . than in his prose-writings" must not be used to contest that.[9] But the early poems remain of interest, even when they have no lasting value, because they show a different side of Swift, or use a different manner, from that of the prose, because in them Swift's emotions and concerns, hopes and anxieties, are exposed more openly than he generally permitted himself in prose.

II

Swift turned to Cowley expecting the distinction of writing in a noble poetic form, the permanence of an ancient tradition, and the assistance of established models. Cowley claimed that the ode was "the noblest and highest kind of writing in Verse,"[10] and Cowley himself was regarded, during Swift's youth, as "the worthy successor and rival of . . . the Ancients."[11] Swift's admiration for Cowley's odes is attested to in a footnote, almost surely literally true, to *The Battle of the Books*: "I think *Cowley's* Pindaricks are much preferable to his *Mistress*."[12] He took his work as a poet, in the early 1690s, very seriously. He studied poetry two hours a morning, "when the humor sits, which I esteem for the flower of the whole Day"; he worked carefully—seldom writing more than two stanzas a week and altering them a hundred times—and yet did not believe himself "to be a laborious dry writer."[13] He shows the enthusiasm and dedication of one who, in poetry as well as in social and economic position, is pushing his "advancement with all the eagerness and courage imaginable, and [does] not doubt to succeed."[14]

Cowley's Pindarics, however, did not provide the formal structure Swift required. Cowley knew the structural principles of Pindar's odes, but he did not choose to follow them. He concentrated, instead, on reproducing in English the "Stile & Manner" of Pindar; in doing so, however, he apprehended only a part of Pindar's distinctive quality. Robert Shafer described that distinctiveness as follows: "Pindar's ruggedness, his swiftness, his concentrated expression—all these things unite to produce the emotional effect of unconquerable strength in his poetry. . . . But . . . Pindar's strength is coupled with another characteristic equally prominent—that of loftiness. And loftiness of the true kind cannot be attained without reserve, without self-control and careful discipline."[15] It was apparently a desire for "loftiness" (what the next century would call "sublimity") that led Swift to choose Cowley as his principal model rather than Dryden: his ambitions pointed him toward the sublime rather than the stately. In Pindar himself Swift would have found that loftiness combined with the control and discipline needed by his nature and his literary inexperience. "Every one of [Pindar's] odes is," according to R. C. Jebb, "a work of the most elaborate and complex art, calculated and refined to the smallest detail."[16] That was not, ironically for Swift, the case with the Cowleyan ode.

The most distinctive characteristic of the "Pindaric" tradition originating with Cowley is irregularity. Cowley adopted for his odes the predecessor of modern free verse, with irregular meter and rhyme, which was already an established tradition in English poetry.[17] In the ode, Cowley called for "*Numbers . . .* various and irregular," which, in Sprat's words, are appropriate to all subjects and afford "more various delight" to the mind.[18] Cowley discussed and illustrated his theory in his "Ode. Upon Liberty":

> The more Heroique strain let others take,
> Mine the Pindarique way I'le make.
> The Matter shall be Grave, the Numbers loose and free.
> It shall not keep one setled pace of Time,
> In the same Tune it shall not always Chime,
> Nor shall each day just to his Neighbour Rhime,
> A thousand Liberties it shall dispense,
> And yet shall mannage all without offence;
> Or to the sweetness of the Sound, or greatness of the Sence,
> Nor shall it never from one Subject start,
> Nor seek Transitions to depart,
> Nor its set way o're Stiles and Bridges make,
> Nor thorough Lanes a Compass take
> As if it fear'd some trespass to commit,
> When the wide Air's a Road for it.

Besides freedom of form, the seventeenth-century ode was characterized by boldly imaginative metaphors. Dryden declares that "the Soul" of the Pindaric form "consists in the Warmth and Vigor of Fancy, the masterly Figures, and the copiousness of Imagination."[19] Sprat comments on the boldness of Pindar's metaphors, while Cowley also characterizes the figures of his own Pindarics as "unusual and *bold*, even to *Temeritie*, and such as I durst not have to do withal in any other kinde of *Poetry*." Swift, in writing his odes, had as precedent such passages as

> We break up *Tombs* with *Sacrilegious hands*;
> Old *Rubbish* we remove;
> To walk in *Ruines*, like vain *Ghosts*, we love,

> And with fond *Divining Wands*
>   We search among the *Dead*
>   For Treasures *Buried*,
> Whilst still the *Liberal Earth* does hold
> So many *Virgin Mines* of *undiscover'ed Gold*.
>   (Cowley, "To Mr. Hobs," 41–48)

Most of Cowley's successors in the ode lacked his metaphysical
bent. Their imagery, all too often, surprises by its ingenuity
rather than by its striking appropriateness and lacks the unity
through emotion which Cowley at his best did achieve. Finally,
the ode was characterized by elevated flights of imagination and
majesty of thought. Cowley told those who were displeased with
the levity of *The Mistress* that they might content their "more
serious inclinations in the weight and height of the ensuing Arguments." Again, Cowley's followers in the tradition undercut
his precept by uninspired treatments of uninspiring topics. The
freedom of form permitted a wide variety of subject matter, as
Sprat noted: "If the irregularity of the number disgust [any],
they may observe that this very thing makes that kind of Poesie
fit for all manner of subjects: For the Pleasant, the Grave, the
Amorous, the Heroic, the Philosophical, the Moral, the Divine." By the latter part of the seventeenth century any irregular
poem which avoided "common speech" could be a "Pindaric."[20]
Charles Cotton developed treatises about women and beauty
and labeled them Pindaric odes; Mrs. Behn wrote "Pindaric"
panegyrics following quite unexalted pastoral conventions; and
Thomas Flatman produced "Pindaric" vignettes called "The Retirement" and "The Disappointed." And the majority of the
panegyrics—which became the main use of the "Pindaric" form
by Flatman, Oldham, Shadwell, Tate, and Katherine Phillips,
to name just a few of its better-known users—lack both weight
and height.

These, then, are the conventions Swift attempted to follow in
his first efforts as a poet. His odes are irregular, perhaps the most
complex of any seventeenth-century poet's:

Sing (belov'd Muse) the Pleasures of Retreat,
    And in some untouch'd Virgin Strain
Shew the Delights thy Sister Nature yields,
Sing of thy Vales, sing of thy Woods, sing of thy Fields;
      Go publish o'er the Plain
    How mighty a Proselyte you gain!
How noble a Reprisal on the Great!
      How is the Muse luxuriant grown,
        Whene'er she takes this Flight
        She soars clear out of sight,
These are the Paradises of her own;
(The Pegasus, like an unruly Horse
      Tho' ne'er so gently led
To the lov'd Pasture where he us'd to feed,
Runs violently o'er his usual Course.)
    Wake from thy wanton Dreams,
    Come from thy dear-lov'd Streams,
    The crooked Paths of wandering *Thames.*
    Fain the fair Nymph would stay,
    Oft she looks back in vain,
    Oft 'gainst her Fountain does complain,
And softly steals in many Windings down,
As loth to see the hated Court and Town,
    And murmurs as she glides away.
      ("Ode to Sir William Temple," IX)

The complexity here does not result from the unruliness of Swift's soaring muse or the complexity of the thought he is communicating. Swift's irregularity is artificial, a failure to suit his form to his thought. He does introduce bold metaphors, as in the passage above, but his figures lack warmth and vigor; they lack emotional immediacy and depend mostly on intellectual impact. Swift does seek an elevated treatment of a dignified theme, but lacking Cowley's ability to give his theme life through a series of conceits, he attempts to add universal significance by associating the subject with a broad abstraction and devoting a good share of the poem to development of that theme. Unfortunately, discourses on "Doing Good," "Virtue," and "Truth" lack the fervor, the core of emotion, on which Cowley depends to elevate his style.

In his first choice of a model, Swift, misjudging his talents or thinking wishfully, chose unwisely. Cowley's example imposed few restraints upon Swift; it did not lead him to discipline and shape his material. In retrospect, looking back across his entire career, one can see he had no hope of succeeding in this first venture; perhaps because of his constitutional need for order, for a sense of direction and a feeling of control in life as well as in art, Swift's successful works nearly always follow or parody a literary model which provides limitations and a fairly definite structural pattern.[21]

III

In addition to experimenting with literary forms, Swift in his odes was also learning to use allusions. Although he alluded frequently to his principal model, Cowley, these allusions are almost all incidental, merely verbal.[22] Later in his career Swift would have organized them to reinforce an idea or to establish a tone, rather than using them randomly and in passing. The odes are of interest in showing Swift struggling toward a more purposeful handling of allusions, but the first successes in such use of allusions are more than a decade away.

All of Swift's odes use allusions freely, probably following the example of Cowley. Like Pindar before him, Cowley sought to achieve brevity and variety in his odes by bringing in scattered, often brief, allusions to a wide variety of works; and Swift does likewise. In his earliest poem, "Ode to the King," Swift scatters a variety of echoes or allusions without order or unity—to Cowley, Shakespeare, Spenser, Dryden, the Bible, and various classical works and figures. Typical is this mixture of metaphors and echoes of Dryden and the classics:

The *Giddy Brittish Populace*,
     That *Tyrant-Guard* on *Peace*,
     Who watch Her like a Prey,
And keep Her for a Sacrifice,
And must be sung, like *Argus*, into *ease*
Before this *Milk-white Heifer* can be stole away,
     Our *Prince* has charm'd its many hundred Eyes;
     Has lull'd the Monster in a Deep
     And (I hope) an Eternal Sleep.
                              ("Ode to the King," 72–80)

The metamorphosis of Peace from a "Prey" to a "Sacrifice" and then to Io combines markedly differing connotations and would be difficult to grasp even with a less convoluted syntax. The complex of Christian and classical overtones that line 77 would inevitably carry in 1690—from the "Milk-white Hind," symbolizing the Catholic Church,[23] and the classical "*Heifer*"—adds to the confusion, for the combination is not natural and purposeful. And to portray the British people as Argus with "its many hundred Eyes" is forced, for the Argus story and its overtones neither fit Swift's passage or meaning nor clarify or reinforce his theme. His use of allusions seems, at this point, an affectation designed to impress rather than to enlighten, and this is entirely in accord with the spirit of a young poet whose earliest extant poem is addressed to the king.

Something of the same tendency remains in the "Ode to the Athenian Society." The same mixture of Christian and classical appears, as the opening biblical allusion to the Deluge is fused with the classical by a substitution of Parnassus for Ararat and the locating of Parnassus "nigh to Heaven":

As when the *Deluge* first began to fall,
     That *mighty Ebb* never to flow again,
     (When this huge Bodies Moisture was so great
It quite o'recame the vital Heat,)
That Mountain which was highest first of all
Appear'd, above the Universal Main,

> To bless the *Primitive Sailer*'s weary sight,
> And 'twas perhaps *Parnassus*, if in height
>   It be as great as 'tis in Fame,
>   And nigh to Heaven as is its Name.
>   (1–10)

The near identification of the Christian and the classical is continued when, in line 26, the biblical Ararat replaces Parnassus, while Noah's dove becomes a *"Dove-muse"* (16) and returns with not an olive leaf but a *"Laurel* branch" (27). Again, there is a prolixity of differing allusions in the comparison of the biblical Eden and the classical Delos to Ireland:

> As if the Universal *Nile*
> Had rather water'd it, than drown'd:
> It seems some floating piece of *Paradice*,
>   Preserv'd by wonder from the Flood,
> Long *wandring thrô the Deep*, as we are told
>   Fam'd *Delos* did of old,
> And the transported Muse imagin'd it
> To be a fitter *Birth-place for the God of Wit.*
>   (42–49)

But the allusions here are at least more functional than in the previous passage. They introduce and are unified by the society's dual concerns with secular and religious wisdom. The allusion to the Deluge introduces the idea of a new beginning, purged of previous evil and inadequacy, blessed by God's approval and favor; while the allusions to Parnassus, suggesting intellectual and artistic excellence, and even to Delos, birthplace of the god of the civilizing virtues, are purposeful and appropriate.

The "Ode to Sir William Temple" is filled with allusions to Cowley. It is as if Swift, seeking to do his utmost to honor his patron, invokes Cowley's "muse" in a vain hope that the master's boldness and strength will accompany it:

> How is the Muse luxuriant grown,
>   Whene'er she takes this Flight

> She soars clear out of sight,
> These are the Paradises of her own;
> (The Pegasus, like an unruly Horse
>   Tho' ne'er so gently led
> To the lov'd Pasture where he us'd to feed,
> Runs violently o'er his usual Course.)
>   (142–49)

The passage echoes these lines in Cowley's "The Resurrection":

> Stop, stop, my *Muse*, allay thy vig'rous heat,
>   Kindled at a *Hint* so Great.
> Hold thy *Pindarique Pegasus* closely in,
>   Which does to *rage* begin,
> And this steep *Hill* would gallop up with violent course,
> 'Tis an unruly, and a *hard-Mouth'd Horse*,
>   Fierce, and unbroken yet,
>   Impatient of the *Spur* or *Bit*.
>   (52–59)

Lash it as he may, however, Swift's muse refuses to become unruly, let alone to rage. He uses noticeably fewer metaphors in the "Ode to Sir William Temple" than in the other odes and noticeably more similes: because he lacked the emotional fervor which created the startlingly correct fusion of vehicle and tenor in Cowley's conceits, he turned increasingly to the explicit comparisons which reason can establish without the help of emotion. When he does produce powerful and effective metaphors, they are, significantly, in satiric passages:

> Our Knowledge is but mere Remembrance all,
>   Remembrance is our Treasure and our Food;
> Nature's fair Table-book our tender Souls
> We scrawl all o'er with old and empty Rules,
>   Stale Memorandums of the Schools;
>   For Learning's mighty Treasures look
>   In that deep Grave a Book,
>   Think she there does all her Treasures hide,
> And that her troubled Ghost still haunts there since she dy'd.
>   ("Ode to Temple," 30–38)

Although emotion, power, and elevation appear in some passages of the ode to Temple, the work as a whole lacks the emotional force to unify the variety of topics it takes up: virtue, learning, peace, designing politicians, pastoral retreat, and the tyranny of the muse. Swift deeply desired to praise Temple, but something held him back. Preoccupied with formal problems in this and the other odes, he failed to realize that there is also the problem of honesty—that his reason, by instinct or theological training, prevented him from giving the unreserved adulation the genre demands. The halting and tentative experiments with allusion in the odes took Swift toward a technique which would unify structure and theme, but it was not yet successful, and would not be until he returned to it several years later in a different kind of poetry.

IV

The odes, besides illustrating Swift's struggles with his own temperament, structure, and allusions, also reveal the effect of his training and inclination. The clergyman and moralist in Swift give his odes a distinctive structure and tone, not necessarily more appealing for their distinctiveness. Lacking Cowley's ability to convey a significant meaning through a series of conceits and thus to give his theme vitality, Swift sought lasting significance by associating his particular subjects with larger themes, universalized abstractions. Only Swift among the many writers of Pindarics during the late seventeenth century employs such a strategy, one which may very well relate to his training in homiletics.

The reform in preaching style during the Restoration included the introduction of a simplified sermon structure: explication, confirmation, application. Swift's own sermon style is quite relaxed even in its use of that structure. His introductions do not so much explicate a text as elaborate on the topic introduced by the text. He does not separate his confirmation and application explicitly, but develops his topic through a two- to four-part analysis which combines the confirmation and application. We

have, of course, only later sermons to judge by and no way of
knowing if his method was the same earlier in his career. Yet it
is interesting that the construction of the odes, as well as their
intent, resembles closely that of his sermons.

The opening lines of the odes correspond to the text of a sermon, as in the "Ode to the King":

> Sure there's some Wondrous Joy in *Doing Good*;
>   Immortal Joy, that suffers no Allay from Fears.
>
> (1–2)

The remainder of the first stanza and often the second as well
amplify that text:

> But the Delight of *Doing Good*
> Is fix't like Fate among the Stars,
>   And Deifi'd in Verse;
> 'Tis the best Gemm in Royalty,
>   The Great Distinguisher of Blood,
>   Parent of Valour and of Fame,
>   Which makes a Godhead of a Name,
> And is Contemporary to Eternity.
>
> (19–26)

Then follows a statement of the thesis to be developed:

> These are the Ways
> By which our happy Prince carves out his Bays;
>   Thus he has fix'd His Name
> First, in the mighty List of Fame.
>
> (31–34)

The stanzas following defend and illustrate that thesis, much as
the points of a sermon enlarge upon its topic. The "Ode to Sir
William Temple," for example, which announces the topic of
"Virtue" and sets forth the thesis that "We have too long been
led astray, . . . 'Tis you must put us in the Way" (17,20), ampli-
fies this theme in three points: Virtue is not found in abstract
learning, but Temple combines the traits of "Learn'd, Good,

and Great" (III–IV); Virtue is not found in politics and war, though Temple maintained his virtue to the end in the midst of them (V–VIII); virtues and pleasures can, however, be found in a pastoral retreat, such as that which Temple is enjoying (IX–XI).

The "Ode to Dr. William Sancroft" begins in much the same way, with text and amplification:

> Truth is eternal, and the Son of Heav'n,
> 　　Bright effluence of th' immortal ray,
> 　. 　. 　. 　. 　. 　. 　. 　. 　. 　.
> 　First of God's darling attributes,
> 　　Thou daily seest Him face to face,
> Nor does thy essence fix'd depend on giddy circumstance
> 　　Of time or place,
> Two foolish guides in ev'ry sublunary dance:
> 　How shall we find Thee . . . .
> 　　　　　　(1–10)

The thesis is outlined in the following two stanzas:

> But where is ev'n thy Image on our earth?
> 　. 　. 　. 　. 　. 　. 　. 　. 　. 　.
> No wonder, then, we talk amiss
> Of truth, and what, or where it is:
> 　. 　. 　. 　. 　. 　. 　. 　. 　.
> Ill may I live, if the good SANCROFT in his holy rest,
> 　　In the divin'ty of retreat,
> 　Be not the brightest pattern Earth can shew
> 　　Of heav'n-born Truth below.
> 　　　　(17, 41–42, 50–53)

What follows, however, is not the reasoned discourse of the preacher, telling "the People what is their Duty; and then [convincing] them that it is so,"[24] though a rough pattern of development can be discerned: chastisement of those who choose ambition and political power over Sancroft's example of living for Truth (IV–V); attack on the vacillation and corruption of the world and especially of England (VI–VII); praise of Sancroft as a heaven-sent guide to his fellow men on earth (VIII–IX); and regret that the church has forced Sancroft into retreat, thus depriving the world of his influence and example (X–XI). The voice is not that of a preacher or satirist but that of a prophet proclaiming the vengeance of God. Swift urges the muse:

> Rather put on thy anger and thy spight,
>   And some kind pow'r for once dispense
> Thro' the dark mass, the dawn of so much sense,
> To make them understand, and feel me when I write;
>   The muse and I no more revenge desire,
> Each line shall stab, shall blast, like daggers and like fire.
>   (86–91)

The role of prophet is reinforced by the many biblical allusions, which blend nicely with the form and tone into some of the most unified and interesting poetry in the odes. Besides such general religious references as "Heaven's dusky shade" (21), "the divin'ty of retreat" (51), and "his sacred influence" (153), there are many directly Christian phrases: "Some . . . seek Heaven's high Son / In Caesar's court, or in Jerusalem" (166–67); "Among proud Doctors and disputing Pharisees" (169); "In a vile manger laid, / And foster'd in a wretched inn" (174–75); "like his Master's Crown, inwreath'd with thorn" (200); "Where the bless'd spirit lodges like the dove" (227); "to heavenly soil transplanted" (228). In addition are the direct verbal parallels: "The brightest pattern Earth can shew" (52) to Titus 2:7, "In all things shewing thyself a pattern of good works"; "In his own balance, false and light" (55) to Proverbs 11:1, "A false balance is abomination to the Lord"; "Death's sting is swallow'd up in victory at last" (201) to 1 Corinthians 15:55, "O death, where is thy sting? O grave, where is thy victory?"; "The bitter cup is from him past" (202) to Matthew 26:42, "He went away again the second time, and prayed, saying, O my Father, if this cup may not pass away from me, except I drink it, thy will be done." The most interesting of these allusions are echoes of the prophets. "Pronounc'd" (119,

120), which is used over and over by Jeremiah, invokes in Swift's poem and age the spirit of Jeremiah's message to Israel: "For the Lord of hosts, that planted thee, hath pronounced evil against thee, for the evil of the house of Israel and of the house of Judah."[25] Similarly, "ruin'd" (178), "laid waste" (178), and "opprest" (186) contribute to the tone Swift is seeking, the voice of one crying in the wilderness, "Repent ye."

Swift's inability to finish the ode to Sancroft[26] provides the final evidence that he was not suited by talent or temperament to the Great Ode, or to panegyric in general. The prophetic tone perhaps suggests the reason for his failure in these poems of praise. References to sin and punishment abound; the "Ode to Sancroft" is deeply imbued with a sense of evil, of the rank British soil that needs cleansing:

> Ah, BRITAIN, land of angels! which of all thy sins,
> . . . .
> Has given thee up a dwelling-place to fiends?
>   Sin and the plague ever abound
> In governments too easy, and too fruitful ground.
>   (92–97)

The two previous odes focus equally on man's condition. The "Ode to the Athenian Society" stresses "the *Worlds Disease*, / (That Epidemick Error and Depravity / Or in our Judgment or our Eye)" (138–40), while the "Ode to Sir William Temple" begins with an allusion to the Fall: "Virtue, the greatest of all Monarchies, / Till its first Emperor rebellious Man / Depos'd from off his Seat . . ." (1–3). Swift's consciousness of evil in man prevented him from writing unqualified encomiums, as Kathryn Montgomery Harris has argued convincingly: "The nature of man has made unequivocal praise impossible. When encountered . . . panegyric must be suspect; when attempted, its validity must depend upon a tempering dose of reality or the overwhelming opposition of fools."[27] It is not just that Swift included satiric passages—for other panegyrists had done so before him[28]—but

rather that Swift consistently defines positive values by contrast
to negative ones and qualifies his praise with guarded reserva-
tions:

> If all that our weak knowledge titles virtue, be
> (High Truth) the best resemblance of exalted Thee,
>   If a mind fix'd to combat fate
> With those two pow'rful swords, Submission and Humility,
>   Sounds truly good, or truly great;
> Ill may I live, if the good SANCROFT in his holy rest,
>   In the divin'ty of retreat,
>   Be not the brightest pattern Earth can shew
>   Of heav'n-born Truth below:
> But foolish Man still judges what is best
>   In his own balance, false and light,
>   Foll'wing Opinion, dark, and blind,
>   That vagrant leader of the mind,
> Till Honesty and Conscience are clear out of sight.
>   ("Ode to Sancroft," 45–58)

This stanza, which includes the poem's highest praise of Sancroft,
opens with an "If," which qualifies the entire assertion about
Sancroft as exemplar of Truth; "our weak knowledge" reminds
us of man's limitations, as does "fate," which can be combated
only by heroes. The praise of Sancroft's truth is followed, almost
climactically, by an exposure of the contrary—"foolish Man,"
with his darkness and blindness. Swift will eventually come to
write successful works of praise,[29] but it will usually be through
raillery or irony, where the form reminds one of faults and weaknesses even as it praises virtues and strengths. His reluctance to
praise unreservedly, deeply ingrained by both temperament and
training, made inevitable Swift's failure in panegyric and in the
Great Ode, and it led, just as inevitably, in his prose, to expansion of the homiletic tone and intentions that gave shape to the
odes.

V

The shift from the irregular ode to the heroic couplets of "To Mr. Congreve" signals Swift's recognition of that failure. He protests, tongue-in-cheek, that this poem also was to be panegyric:

> Perish the Muse's hour, thus vainly spent
> In satire, to my CONGREVE's praises meant.
>
> (175–76)

But Swift acknowledges that he cannot be a "grave adviser" (202) and that he cannot adhere to his "first intent" (201) of praising Congreve straightforwardly. Satire is the actual, if not avowed, intent; it is the "new address" (17) the Muse advises him to find.

Swift's role as prophet, implicit in the ode to Sancroft, becomes explicit in the poem to Congreve. The opening line announces that he called the Muse with "a prophet's voice and prophet's pow'r." Only Congreve's merits have restrained "*my resentment's weight*" (46) and averted, so far, "*th'impending judgments of my pen*" (48). But those judgments will come, for Swift has now accepted the satirist's traditional calling as prophet:

> *My hate, whose lash just heaven has long decreed*
> *Shall on a day make sin and folly bleed.*
>
> (133–34)

Heaven has appointed him to destroy the "golden calf" (108) of Grub Street rules, to attack the "Babel of the pit" (122), to waken "the bad world" (198) from the dream in which it languishes. Two related but not yet integral and unified allusions confirm that calling. Lines 31–32—"For, youth, believe, to you unseen, is fix'd / A mighty gulph unpassable betwixt"—allude to the story of the Rich Man and Lazarus (Luke 16:19–31). Between the Rich Man, suffering in hell's flames, and Lazarus, lying in Abraham's bosom, "there is a great gulf fixed." The Rich Man begs that Lazarus be sent to warn his brothers about this place of torment, to which Abraham replies, "If they hear not Moses and the prophets, neither will they be persuaded, though one rose from the dead." Swift is called to be one of those prophets, to warn the rich and corrupt of his day of the fate in store for them. The other key allusion is to Acts 10:9–16, where Peter, in a vision, sees

a certain vessel descending unto him, as it had been a great sheet knit at the four corners, and let down to the earth: wherein were all manner of fourfooted beasts of the earth, and wild beasts, and creeping things, and fowls of the air. And there came a voice to him, Rise, Peter; kill, and eat. But Peter said, Not so, Lord; for I have never eaten any thing that is common or unclean. And the voice spake unto him again the second time, What God hath cleansed, that call not thou common.

This episode is one of the most significant in the history of the early church, for in it Peter is told to go out and prophesy to the Gentiles. The Gentiles, hitherto to be avoided like unclean foods, were now to be ministered to and brought to repentance. Swift draws that story into the final lines of his poem:

> In this descending sheet you'll haply find
> Some short refreshment for your weary mind,
> Nought it contains is common or unclean,
> And once drawn up, is ne'er let down again.

The allusion is highly suggestive for a poem that has listed a wide variety of unclean animals—the "cattle" referred to twice (116, 224), the "*chatt'ring throng*" (223), "*th'offensive herd*" with "*odious smell and sight*" (226, 225). The lines specifically assert the purity and value of Swift's art in the poem, but they also imply that Swift too is being sent, to drive off the "swarms of gnats" that "can rob the world of day" (81–82), to expose the "city butter-fly" for the "worm" it really is (89–90), and to strip off "the lion's skin" that conceals the ass (172).

The animal imagery, the theme of Grub Street literature and its social implications, the emphasis on the "transitory" (128) and "volatile" (209) nature of the world, and the fable of the lad who went to the city and, "having cast his coat, and well pursu'd / The methods most in fashion to be lewd," came back "a finish'd spark" (115–46) all anticipate *A Tale of a Tub*. Whether Swift could foresee this in 1693 or not, whether he had already begun work on the *Tale* or not, that was the form "*th'impending judgments of* [his] *pen*" were to take. Further efforts in Pindaric or heroic verse would obviously be futile: Swift knew now what he later put into words, that nothing is so hard to write as serious praise.[30] For Swift it was even harder than for most. In "To Mr. Congreve," purportedly a tribute to Congreve's fame—"the greatest compliment she [the Muse] ever made" (28)—Congreve is praised only by indirection, by his *not* being one of the Grub Street fools attacked throughout the poem. Although Swift addresses the Muse all through the poem and quotes her in reply, he realizes that he must part company with her. She is "*sham'd and amaz'd*" (223) for the society and creatures which Swift, to expose, must get to know; the Muse, he admits, "*does th'offensive herd avoid*" (226).

In "To Mr. Congreve" Swift comes to the realization that he and the Muse must part in order for his talents to develop as they should; in the lines "Occasioned by Sir W—— T——'s Late Illness and Recovery" (1693), the parting takes place. First there is a tender backward glance to their first meeting:

> Late near yon whisp'ring stream,
> Where her own TEMPLE was her darling theme;
> There first the visionary sound was heard,
> When to poetic view the Muse appear'd.
> (13–16)

Then comes the parting, harsher perhaps than she deserves who has shared so many hours esteemed "for the flower of the whole Day."

> Malignant goddess! bane to my repose,
> Thou universal cause of all my woes.
>   (81–82)

It is not only a dismissal but a disenchantment, a total rejection of her presence and value:

> Madness like this no fancy ever seiz'd,
> Still to be cheated, never to be pleas'd;
> .   .   .   .
> There thy enchantment broke, and from this hour
> I here renounce thy visionary pow'r;
> And since thy essence on my breath depends,
> Thus with a puff the whole delusion ends.
>   (147–54)

Swift's affair with the Muse is over. He will continue "to mistaken man these truths [to] rehearse, / Who dare revile the integrity of verse" (69–70), but, his reason now awake (99), he will do so first in a different medium—prose—and later in quite a different manner of verse.[31]

The period of the odes and heroic verse was in large part one of self-discovery for Swift. It was a period of experimenting to determine what literary modes his particular combination of talents, temperament, and interests were best suited to. Swift did not in these years discover what he could do in verse, but he did learn what he could not do. He discovered themes which seemed vital to him and which, though he could not develop them fully in poetry, were to be the heart of his first and most brilliant prose work. And although he did not solve the problem of reconciling structure, theme, and tone through the use of allusions, his groping efforts started him toward the solution he was to find in a very different type of poetry several years later.

II

Needy Poet Seeking for Aid
The First Verse Satires

I

A convenient way to discuss the development of Swift's poetic style is to compare the two versions of "Vanbrug's House": the manuscript version, dated 1703, and the version published in the *Miscellanies* of 1711, but dated 1708 in Faulkner's edition.[1] The poetical and rhetorical techniques which Swift combined into a distinctive style of verse did not spring forth fully grown when the odes were allowed a quiet passing. The dates of composition and revision of "Vanbrug's House," a playful satire on architect and dramatist John Vanbrugh, nearly span the years in which Swift was finding his poetic voice. Improved handling of wit, the introduction of dialogue and dramatic effects, and a humor, a stronger and more subtle satiric attack, and greater depth of theme than the manuscript version. The early version typifies Swift's first, hesitant efforts in tetrameters; the revised version anticipates the distinctive style of Swift's finest later poems.

The opening verse paragraph of the revised poem differs little
from that of the earlier version:

> In Times of Old, when Time was *Young*,
> And Poets their own Verses Sung,
> A Verse could draw a Stone or Beam
> That now would overload a Team;
> Lead 'em a Dance of many a Mile,
> Then rear 'em to a goodly Pile.
> Each Number had it's diff'rent Pow'r;
> Heroick Strains could build a Tow'r;
> Sonnets, or Elogies to *Chloris*
> Might raise a House about two Stories;
> A Lyrick Ode would Slate; a Catch
> Would Tile; an Epigram would Thatch.
>
> (B, 1–12)

Swift apparently chose tetrameters, after his lack of success with
the ode and pentameters, because he was no longer attempting
to compete with the serious writers of heroic couplets. Instead,
he was placing himself in the lighter, but by no means frivolous,
tradition of tetrameter verse of the latter half of the seventeenth
century. On the lighter side he was influenced, obviously, by
Samuel Butler, but also by William King; on the more serious
side, by Ben Jonson.[2] Swift combines, then, the raciness and ir-
reverence of the former and the terseness and regularity of the
latter into a style capable of fierce, earnest attack or trivial, personal tomfoolery, but never of grave dignity. He had in Jonson
an example of one who used the heroic line for serious efforts
and tetrameters often for lighter verse. Henceforth for Swift,
weighty matters would be handled in prose—it might be judged
by the sternest standards; his verse in tetrameters was to be
judged by other standards, as the supposedly casual product of
leisure hours—serious at times, yes, but never solemn or dignified.

Revisions in the succeeding verse paragraphs indicate the first
major development in Swift's technique, a shift to a greater emphasis on wit. Lines 13–14 of the manuscript, for example—

"Now Poets find this Art is lost, / Both to their own and Land-
lord's Cost"—become, in the printed poem,

> But, to their own, or Landlord's Cost,
> Now Poets feel this Art is lost.
> (B, 13-14)

The revision is smoother metrically, and the inversion enhances
the central idea by delaying it. The changes in the next couplet
are similar:

> Not one of all the tunefull Throng
> Can hire a Lodging for a Song.
> (A, 15-16)

> Not one of all our tuneful Throng
> Can raise a Lodging *for a Song*.
> (B, 15-16)

The pun on "raise" retains the earlier meaning but adds a very
appropriate second meaning. More extensive changes appear in
the next three couplets:

> For Jove consider'd well the Case,
> That Poets were a numerous Race,
> And if they all had Power to build,
> The Earth would very soon be filld:
> Materials would be quickly spent,
> And Houses would not give a Rent.
> (A, 17-22)

> For, *Jove* consider'd well the Case,
> Observ'd, they grew a num'rous Race.
> And should they *Build* as fast as *Write*,
> 'Twould ruin Undertakers quite.
> (B, 17-20)

The change to "*grew* a num'rous Race" substitutes an active
verb for a lifeless one and expands the satiric implications by
suggesting that the profusion of poets and the rapidity with

which their works proliferated were a recent and pernicious development, rather than just a long-standing but previously unrecognized problem. Since the most potent and witty of the consequences given in the first version was the last, the economic one, Swift condenses three lines to one, a sharp satiric jab at the attitude which values producer above consumer. He also adds two lines which set up Jove's action nicely:

> This Evil, therefore to prevent,
> He wisely chang'd their Element.
>
> (B, 21–22)

Lines 23–28, which from the first provided a witty conclusion to the poem's basic myth, needed little change:

> On Earth, the God of Wealth was made
> Sole Patron of the Building Trade,
> Leaving the Wits the Spacious Air
> With Licence to *build Castles* there:
> And 'tis conceiv'd, their old Pretence
> To lodge in Garrats, comes from thence.
>
> (B, 23–28)

But the next twenty-six lines (29–54) were omitted entirely, in one of the most important of the deletions.

> There is a Worm by Phœbus bred,
> By Leaves of Mulberry is fed;
> Which unprovided where to dwell,
> Consumes it self to weave a Cell.
> Then curious Hands this Texture take,
> And for themselves fine Garments make.
> Mean time a Pair of awkward Things
> Grew to his Back instead of Wings;
> He flutters when he Thinks he flyes,
> Then sheds about his Spaun, and dyes.
> Just such an Insect of the Age
> Is he that scribbles for the Stage.
>
> (A, 29–40)

The account of Phoebus's worm is not closely related to the central myth of the poem, that of the poet building *by means of* his poetry, and the application to modern drama is painfully obvious and heavy-handed. The focus is narrow, dealing only with a temporary, local situation and lacking the universal implications that give poetry lasting interest. The style lacks variety: its overly regular rhythm, paucity of caesuras, slow pace, and closed couplets—all typical of Swift's other early tetrameters—contrast sharply with his later style. The revised poem omits this entire passage and proceeds directly to lines 55–58 of the manuscript version:

> Premising thus in Modern way
> The greater half I had to say,
> Sing Muse the House of Poet Van
> In higher Strain than we began.

The only revisions made in these lines are the use of the initial "V" for "Van" and the substitution of "better" for "greater" in line 56. To this point, then, the revisions have been mostly minor, but they have marked an important new emphasis on wit. Like Swift's other early verse satires ("The Discovery," "The Problem," "A Ballad on the Game of Traffick"), the manuscript version of "Van's House" relies for its humor on its situation, not on its handling of particular words, lines, and ideas. By the time of the revision, Swift had learned to gain immediate effects within individual parts of the poem, rather than depending on the entire poem for a total effect.

The second major revision of "Van's House," indicating another aspect of Swift's development as a poet, is strategic, a moving from heavy reliance on narrative to considerable use of dramatic techniques. The account of Van as builder in the manuscript is simple narrative:

> Van, (for 'tis fit the Reader know it)
> Is both a Herald and a Poet;
> No wonder then, if nicely skill'd

In each Capacity to Build:
As Herald, he can in a Day
Repair a House gone to decay;
Or by Atchievments, Arms, Device
Erect a new one in a Trice;
And Poets if they had their Due,
By antient Right are Builders too.
This made him to Apollo pray
For Leave to build the Poet's Way.

.   .   .   .

After hard Throws of many a Day
Van was deliver'd of a Play,
Which in due time brought forth a House;
Just as the Mountain did the Mouse;
One Story high, one postern Door,
And one small Chamber on a Floor.
                              (A, 59–78)

The published version retains lines 59–66 essentially unchanged, but then substitutes the lines which turn "Van's House" into an excellent comic poem. For the simple narration of the manuscript, Swift substitutes a dramatic vignette, with Van stating his ideas directly:

And as a Poet, he has Skill
To build in Speculation still.
Great *Jove*, he cry'd, the Art restore
To build by Verse as heretofore,
And make my Muse the Architect;
What Palaces shall we erect!
                              (B, 41–46)

Swift had employed direct speech very successfully before, in "Mrs. Harris's Petition," but that was a dramatic monologue, and in other early poems he was unable to achieve a lively, natural combination of narrative and dialogue (cf. "The Discovery," "The Problem"). The first successful example of such a combination is the manuscript version of "Baucis and Philemon," in which the traditional story provided a structure that freed Swift to concentrate on characterization and detail. The use of an external source for the broad outlines of his material and of colloquial speech for its development mark "Baucis and Philemon" as an important milestone in Swift's growth as a poet. Those techniques are crucial in the reshaping of "Van's House," and they reappear again and again in the best of his later poems. Van's words continue:

> No longer shall forsaken *Thames*
> Lament his old *Whitehall* in Flames,
> A Pile shall from its Ashes rise
> Fit to Invade or prop the Skies.
>
> (B, 47–50)

The second couplet anticipates two allusions which reappear later in the poem, to the Phoenix and to the Tower of Babel. Whether Van plans to enter heaven, as Nimrod intended, or only to support it, as Atlas had to for his rebellion against the gods, the audacity at least borders on hubris, appropriately enough for one who is "For Building fam'd, and justly reckond / At Court, Vitruvius the second."[3]

The next couplet may be the best of the additions to the poem. The lines in the earlier version—"His Pray'r was granted, for the God / Consented with the usuall Nod" (A, 71–72)—become in the revision,

> *Jove* Smil'd, and like a gentle God,
> Consenting with the usual Nod,
> Told V—— he knew his Talent best,
> And left the Choice to his own Breast.
>
> (B, 51–54)

Out of vague, lifeless descriptive lines Swift has created a tiny dramatic scene, carrying into his verse a technique which he had used very successfully in *A Tale of a Tub* and which would become characteristic of his best poetry. The drama continues throughout the paragraph:

> So V—— resolv'd to write a Farce,
> But well perceiving Wit was scarce,
> With Cunning that Defect supplies,
> Takes a *French* Play as lawful Prize,
> Steals thence his Plot, and ev'ry Joke,
> Not once suspecting, *Jove* would *Smoak*,
> And, (like a Wag) sat down to Write,
> Would whisper to himself; *A Bite*,
> Then, from the motly mingled Style
> Proceeded to erect his Pile:
> So, Men of old, to gain Renown, did
> Build *Babel* with their Tongues confounded.
>
> (B, 55–66)

The lines bring Van before the reader vividly, pirating French works, chortling as he enjoys his stolen wit, quivering with delight at his cleverness. Jove, whose benign smile in line 51 reduced Van to the pitiful projector he had been labeled in line 42, also comes to life. The line "Not once suspecting, *Jove* would *Smoak*" makes Jove as real as Swift's former tutor, St. George Ashe ("let the bishop of Clogher smoak it if he can"[4]); it almost gives Jove an elbow and a table on which to rest it as he contemplates Van's antics in patient amusement. The lines which follow bring Jove even closer, turning him into a wise but playful father-figure:

> *Jove* saw the Cheat, but thought it best
> To turn the Matter to a Jest;
> Down from *Olympus* Top he Slides,
> Laughing as if he'd burst his Sides:
> Ay, thought the God, are these your Tricks?
> Why then, *old Plays* deserve *old Bricks*,
> And since you're sparing of your Stuff,
> Your Building shall be small enough.
>
> (B, 67–74)

Here, then, in the brief, detailed characterizations, rapid dramatic situations, colloquial speech patterns, and brisk comic tone are

the antecedents of Swift's finest achievements in verse: the self-
portrait in the imitation of the Seventh Epistle of the First Book
of Horace, the opening lines of the final birthday poem to Stella,
the "My female Friends" passage in "Verses on the Death of Dr.
Swift," and the powerful invectives of "The Legion Club." Swift's
poetic style has begun to move toward what it will be at its best.
The overly regular rhythms of the manuscript version are varied,
in the printed poem, by substitutions and caesuras; the pace of
the verse is stepped up by polysyllabic words and run-on couplets; and the cadences are rendered more natural by better word
placement, interjected phrases, and occasional use of direct
speech. Although the style is still hesitant or tedious at times,
it is well on its way toward the colloquial but taut, carefully
controlled, almost regular tetrameter couplets, punctuated occa-
sionally by a double or triple, often comic, rhyme, which characterize Swift's later poems and are epitomized so well in the
playful gibes and parodies of "Directions for a Birth-day Song"
and the wonderfully varied tones of "On Poetry: A Rapsody."
The ingredients of Swift's mature poetry are already present in
1708, awaiting only further practice and an increasingly sophis-
ticated use of sources and allusions.

The third main area of development in Swift's poetry is a fuller
use of the materials he draws upon and alludes to. In construct-
ing his myth of the poet as "maker," literally as well as metaphorically, Swift combines very felicitously the story of Orpheus
with his own fable of the Spider and the Bee.[5] Orpheus, according to tradition, was among the first and best of all poets. It was
to him Apollo first gave the lyre (Hyginus, *Astronomica*, II, 7); he
is listed by Plato among the greatest early poets (*Apology*, 41a);
and his songs were of such sweetness that they governed nature:
"At his sweet strains the rushing torrents' roar was stilled, and,
forgetful of their eager flight, the waters ceased their flow; . . .
the woods came with their birds to him, yea, perched among
the trees they came."[6] Not only animate nature responded.
Source after source cites his ability to affect rocks and stones as

well: "With such songs the bard of Thrace drew the trees, held
beasts enthralled and constrained stones to follow him."[7] It was
an easy step, for William King, from having Orpheus move
rocks to having him erect buildings: "And by the help of pleas-
ing Ditties, / Make Mill-stones run, and build up Cities."[8] And
it was an equally easy step for Swift to ascribe to "Poets" in general, "In Times of *Old*," powers that originally were limited to
Orpheus. This myth, then, stressing the power and influence of
poetry, underlies the opening section of the poem and lines 75–
94 of the revision:

> [Jove] spake, and grudging, lent his Ayd;
> Th' experienc't Bricks that knew their Trade,
> (As being Bricks at Second Hand,)
> Now move, and now in Order Stand.
>
>   The Building, as the Poet Writ,
> Rose in proportion to his Wit:
> And first the Prologue built a Wall
> So wide as to encompass all.
> The Scene, a Wood, produc'd no more
> Than a few Scrubby Trees before.
> The Plot as yet lay deep, and so
> A Cellar next was dug below:
> But this a Work so hard was found,
> Two Acts it cost him under Ground.
> Two other Acts we may presume
> Were spent in Building each a Room;
> Thus far advanc't, he made a shift
> To raise a Roof with Act the Fift.
> The Epilogue behind, did frame
> A Place not decent here to name.

Swift had earlier used building as a metaphor for literature. Like
Van, the Spider in *The Battle of the Books* was an architect who
had both designed and built a mansion of which he was proud,
if not vain: "This large Castle (to shew my Improvements in the
Mathematicks) is all built with my own Hands, and the Materials
extracted altogether out of my own Person."[9] The Spider is called

to account for this claim and is reminded that he, again like Van, had not relied solely on what he found within himself. The Bee comments: "If we may judge of the Liquor in the Vessel by what issues out, You possess a good plentiful Store of Dirt and Poison in your Breast; And, tho' I would by no means, lessen or disparage your genuine Stock of either, yet, I doubt you are somewhat obliged for an Encrease of both, to a little foreign Assistance. Your inherent Portion of Dirt, does not fail of Acquisitions, by Sweepings exhaled from below" (p. 232). That the Bee's analysis of the Spider's castle fits Van's house as well becomes clear as Van's brother poets come to see his masterpiece.

> Now Poets from all Quarters ran
> To see the House of Brother V——:
> Lookt high and low, walkt often round,
> But no such House was to be found;
> One asks the Watermen hard by,
> *Where may the Poets Palace ly?*
> Another, of the *Thames* enquires,
> If he has seen its gilded Spires.
> At length they in the Rubbish spy
> A Thing resembling a Goose Py.
>   (B, 95–104)

Swift's judgment of Vanbrugh as architect and playwright parallels the Bee's of the Spider, as Van's work is reduced, metaphorically, to a chicken coop in a rubbish heap—insignificant, unoriginal, and indistinguishable from all that surrounds it.

The point of the poem is directed beyond just Vanbrugh by the revisions to the closing verse paragraphs. By putting these lines into the mouth of one of Van's fellow poets, Swift undercuts Van with the blame-by-false-praise technique he used throughout *A Tale of a Tub*, and he turns the speaker into a target of the satire at the same time.

> Farther in haste the Poets throng,
> And gaze in silent Wonder long,
> Till one in Raptures thus began
> To praise the Pile, and Builder V——.

> Thrice happy Poet, who may trail
> Thy House about thee like a Snail;
> Or Harness'd to a Nag, at ease
> Take Journies in it like a Chaise;
> Or in a Boat when e're thou wilt
> Canst make it serve thee for a Tilt.
> Capacious House! 'tis own'd by all
> Thou'rt well contriv'd, tho' thou art small;
> For ev'ry Wit in *Britain*'s Isle
> May lodge within thy Spacious Pile.
>   (B, 105–18)

The "author" of *A Tale of a Tub* also had proposed a building to house the wits: "It is intended that a large Academy be erected, capable of containing nine thousand seven hundred forty and three Persons; which by modest Computation is reckoned to be pretty near the current Number of *Wits* in this Island" (p. 41). In his enthusiasm for the number or size of the wits in England, the "author" projected a need for a large hall. The speaker in the poem obviously assesses the space needs of even so large a number of wits much more accurately. He goes on to describe the house in a series of unintentionally reductive similes:

> Like *Bacchus* Thou, as Poets feign,
> Thy Mother burnt, art Born again;
> Born like a *Phœnix* from the Flame,
> But neither *Bulk*, nor *Shape* the same:
> As Animals of largest Size
> Corrupt to Maggots, Worms and Flyes.
> A Type of *Modern* Wit and Style,
> *The Rubbish of an Antient Pile.*
> So *Chymists* boast they have a Pow'r
> From the dead Ashes of a Flow'r
> Some faint Resemblance to produce,
> But not the Virtue, Tast or Juice.
> So *Modern* Rimers wisely *Blast*
> The Poetry of Ages past,

Which after they have overthrown,
They from its Ruins build their own.
(B, 119–34)

In the manuscript version, these similes were ineffective because they were not consistent with the central "building" motif. In the printed poem, however, by giving a long series of unrelated similes to a modern writer, Swift makes the passage effective and fitting. The lines now exemplify the bad art Swift is attacking: the truth of Swift's charges can hardly be disputed in the face of such concrete evidence.

The theme of "Van's House," then, can be stated in the words of Aesop, commenting on the Spider's "great Skill in Architecture" in *The Battle of the Books*: "Erect your Schemes with as much Method and Skill as you please; yet, if the materials be nothing but Dirt, spun out of your own Entrails (the Guts of *Modern* Brains) the Edifice will conclude at last in a *Cobweb*" (p. 234). Vanbrugh and his brother poets are, therefore, further symbols of the modernism attacked in *A Tale of a Tub* and *The Battle of the Books*, of the failure to attain the potential in art for truth and order emphasized by the Orpheus myth or to produce the "Sweetness and Light" mentioned by Aesop in *The Battle of the Books*. In "Van's House" Swift achieved for the first time what would become the characteristic trait of his best poetry: use of allusions or of an external source to expand an initially local or personal situation or incident into a significant statement on art and morality. His handling is still uncertain—the borrowings are actually analogues rather than allusions. He has not yet learned to stay with a source or allusion and weave it throughout the texture of a poem; he cannot yet use sources to shape the tone and theme, as do the allusions to Ovid and Virgil in "Cadenus and Vanessa," or to control structure and meaning, as do allusions to the *Aeneid* and the Bible in "The Legion Club." But a decisive step forward in his development as a poet— in his handling of sources as well as of wit and dramatic techniques—is clear from a comparison of the two versions of "Van's

House." The poem is probably not as good as Bolingbroke said when he called it "the best thing he ever read" (*Journal to Stella*, I, 92); but at least in terms of the study of Swift as a poet, it is important, for it illustrates techniques which would later become characteristic of his best verse and indicates the directions his poetry would take in the future.

II

The development of Swift's use of allusion can be traced in a series of early poems. Earliest is "The Description of a Salamander" (1705), the ideas of which were taken "out of" Pliny. The poem opens innocently enough, justifying a current nickname for a modern war hero. The old labels of lion, eagle, or fox are no longer appropriate because of the invention of guns—"To paint a Hero, we enquire / For something that will conquer Fire" (17–18)—and the label "Salamander" is confirmed as most appropriate for Lord Cutts. The innocent façade continues in the concern shown lest this label be taken as satiric:

> But since we live among
> Detractors with an evil Tongue,
> Who may object against the Term,
> *Pliny* shall prove what we affirm.
>   (23–26)

And the rest of the poem follows closely two sections of Pliny's *Natural History*.

Pliny includes salamanders in his discussion of snakes: "A number of animals spring from some hidden and secret source, even in the quadruped class, for instance salamanders, a creature shaped like a lizard, covered with spots, never appearing except in great rains and disappearing in fine weather."[10] In establishing the genus of the creature in question, Swift follows the outline of this passage closely but adds several damning adjectives not contained in his source:

> First then, our Author has defin'd
> This Reptil, of the Serpent kind,
> With gawdy Coat, and shining Train,
> But loathsom Spots his Body stain:
> Out from some Hole obscure he flies
> When Rains descend, and Tempests rise,
> Till the Sun clears the Air; and then
> Crawls back neglected to his Den.
> (29–36)

The choice of an animal from the serpent class is, of course, inherently incriminating. Without further development of the point, Swift has made Cutts evil, even diabolical. But his main effort is to make physical repulsiveness a metaphor for moral baseness as he applies his figures to Cutts:

> So when the War has rais'd a Storm
> I've seen a *Snake* in human Form,
> All stain'd with Infamy and Vice,
> Leap from the Dunghill in a trice,
> Burnish and make a gaudy show,
> Become a General, Peer and Beau,
> Till Peace hath made the Sky serene,
> Then shrink into it's Hole again.
> (37–44)

Swift attacks Cutts as vain, which he apparently was, and as depraved, which he probably was not. The next few lines take greater liberties with Pliny:

> Farther, we are by *Pliny* told
> This *Serpent* is extreamly cold,
> So cold, that put it in the Fire,
> 'Twill make the very Flames expire.
> (47–50)

Pliny does say in book 10 that the salamander "is so chilly that it puts out fire by its contact, in the same way as ice does," but he later backs away from that claim: "As to the power to protect against fires, which the Magi attribute to the animal, since according to them no other can put fire out, could the salamander really do so, Rome by trial would have already found out. Sextius tells us that as food the salamander, preserved in honey after entrails, feet, and head have been cut away, is aphrodisiac, but he denies its power to put fire out."[11] In any case, selective borrowing from Pliny allows Swift to depict Cutts as cold and hard.

> So have I seen a batter'd Beau
> By Age and Claps grown cold as Snow,
> Whose Breath or Touch, where e'er he came,
> Blew out Love's Torch or chill'd the Flame.
> (57–60)

Swift goes on to his most effective adaptation of Pliny, a fierce attack which grows out of similar lines from two different books. In book 10 Pliny writes that the salamander "vomits from its mouth a milky slaver, one touch of which on any part of the human body causes all the hair to drop off, and the portion touched changes its colour and breaks out in a tetter." And in book 29 Pliny affirms that "all the hair on the whole body falls off if its saliva has sprinkled any part whatever of the body, even the sole of the foot." Swift, by combining Pliny's comments on saliva with the earlier reference to the aphrodisiac qualities ascribed to the salamander, distorts these passages into a devastating sexual attack:

> And should some Nymph who ne'er was cruel,
> Like *Carleton* cheap, or fam'd *Duruel*,
> Receive the Filth which [Cutts] ejects,
> She soon would find, the same Effects,
> Her tainted Carcase to pursue,
> As from the *Salamander's* Spue;
> A dismal shedding of her Locks
> And, if no Leprosy, a Pox.
> (61–68)

The poem illustrates the simplest possible use of a classical model: a line-by-line near-translation, adapting Pliny as a metaphor for moral evil and using Pliny as a vehicle of satiric attack. The external source gives this poem a sureness and smoothness the earlier poems lacked and enables Swift to reach a level of invective he was rarely able to surpass.[12]

The logical step from use of Pliny as a direct source of ideas and development is to a less mechanical travesty, "a free, humorous reworking of a serious narrative which retains the characters and at least a recognizable amount of the subject matter of the original, but reduces everything to the level of bourgeois comedy or farce."[13] This follows soon after "The Description of a Salamander," probably within a year, in "The Story of Baucis and Philemon." The manuscript version of the poem—written, according to a note in the margin, in 1706[14]—has received less critical attention than the revised version published in 1709, but it is the more important in a survey of Swift's artistic development because it represents the first time that Swift used another work to supply an outline for a poem so that he could concentrate on development of the style and details.

A comparison of Swift's poem with Ovid's story, in Dryden's translation,[15] shows that Swift stresses and expands those sections which Ovid passes over briefly, while omitting or summarizing those which Ovid treats at length.

Swift	Ovid
	Setting (1–12)
Introduction (1–4)	Introduction (13–22)
Advent of the two saints in masquerade (5–10)	Advent of Jove and Hermes in disguise (23–26)
They ask for shelter (11–22)	They seek shelter and are denied (27–28)
They are denied, in vivid dialogue (23–46)	

They are admitted by Baucis and Philemon (47–54)

They are admitted by Baucis and Philemon (29–31)

Description of Baucis and Philemon (32–40)

Their welcome by Baucis and Philemon (41–48)

Preparation of the meal (55–72)

Preparation of the meal (48–71)

Washing of the guests' feet (72–76)

Preparation of the table and couches (77–89)

Detailed description of the meal (90–121)

Wine supply renewed (73–82)

Wine supply renewed (122–29)

Attempt to catch the goose (130–41)

Condemnation of neighbors and praise of Baucis and Philemon (83–90)

Condemnation of neighbors and ascent of the mountain (141–51)

Neighborhood turned into a lake (152–56)

Metamorphosis of the cottage into a temple (157–62)

Detailed description of the metamorphosis of the hut into a church (91–152)

Detailed description of the metamorphosis of Philemon into a parson (153–80)

Baucis and Philemon request to be priests and to die together (163–76)

Metamorphosis of Baucis and Philemon into trees (177–90)

Evidence of the truth of the tale: the trees are still standing (191–99)

The differences can be seen both in the relative emphases the same topics receive and in the topics Swift omits entirely. Whereas Ovid devotes almost half the story to details concerning the hospitality of the couple, Swift compresses this to some eighteen lines. On the other hand, Ovid only mentions the metamorphosis of the cottage to a church, giving it five lines, and indicates in passing that Baucis and Philemon served as priests, while Swift devotes exactly half of his 180 lines to a detailed description of those metamorphoses. Ovid, then, places his emphasis on the qualities displayed by Baucis and Philemon in their hospitality and their meal for the gods, which takes on a ritualistic and religious significance, and on the metamorphosis to trees, which symbolizes the providence of the gods. Swift, by compressing the hospitality and the feast and reducing the ultimate transformation to an "&c," turns a symbolic religious tale into a concretely physical report of supposedly actual and literal events.[16]

In travestying Ovid, Swift had available as a model the recent travesty of the story of Orpheus and Euridice, annexed to "Some Remarks on *The Tale of a Tub*." The remarks were written anonymously by William King, whom Swift later helped to the post of Gazetter and called "a Person, who upon some Occasions hath discover'd no ill Vein of Humor" (*A Tale of a Tub*, p. 11), and whose tetrameter couplets, more structured and polished than Butler's, influenced Swift's own. King's opening places the same emphasis on "Story," author, and fairytale qualities as Swift's:

> As Poets say, one *Orpheus* went
> To Hell upon an odd Intent.
> First, tell the Story, then let's know,
> If any one will do so now.[17]

King's poem is even less dependent on Ovid than Swift's and goes even further in transforming the original to his own poem with its own intentions. Although King nominally maintains the antiquity of Orpheus, the language and details are as contemporary as those of Swift's story:

> The Mountains seem'd to bend their Tops,
> And Shutters clos'd the Mill'ners Shops,
> Excluded both the Punks and Fops.
>   (p. 52)

King also relies heavily on dialogue, where it is not justified by Ovid's story, and he too gives it a colloquial verve that adds realism and life to his characters:

> "And then one Rogue cries to another,
> "Since this Wife's gone, e'en get another:
> "Tho most Men let such Thoughts alone,
> "And swear they've had enough of one.
>
> (p. 41)

Realistic detail also appears in the discrepancy in size between Orpheus and the elves and in the procedure advised for Orpheus before he descends to hell:

> Then [Urganda] bid him 'noint himself with Salve;
> Such as those hardy People use,
> Who walk on Fire without their Shoes.
>
> (p. 44)

There is, then, more than a hint for the physical literalization of Ovid, which Swift takes even further, and there is certainly an intent to derive from Ovid a pleasant, humorous tale. Part of the humor in King's poem, as in the opening lines of Swift's, arises from numerous Hudibrastic rhymes: "for't / Court" (p. 41); "jest on / Question" (p. 41); "Pewter / due t'her" (p. 44); and "*Nosnotbocai* / Sulpher choak ye" (p. 53). Finally, it is interesting and perhaps significant that King's poem does not follow Ovid's story to its conclusion, but having, after 415 lines, achieved the desired effects of comedy and travesty, leaves off with an "&c" (p. 63).

Swift's particular method of travesty in "The Story of Baucis and Philemon" is a literalization of Ovid, a reduction of the processes and steps of "metamorphosis" to physical detail and factual representation. Thus, as the "Saints" seek for shelter, their search is given in detail—is even carried out in the rain—and the neighbors turn them down in believably colorful language:

In antient Time, as Story tells
The Saints would often leave their Cells
And strole about, but hide their Quality,
To try the People's Hospitality.
   It happen'd on a Winter's night,
As Authors of the Legend write
Two Brother-Hermits, Saints by Trade
Taking their Tour in Masquerade
Came to a Village hard by Rixham
Ragged, and not a Groat betwixt 'em.
It rain'd as hard as it could pour,
Yet they were forc't to walk an Hour
From House to House, wett to the Skin
Before one Soul would let 'em in.
They call'd at ev'ry Dore; Good People,
My Comrade's Blind, and I'm a Creeple
Here we ly starving in the Street
'Twould grieve a Body's Heart to see't:

.   .   .   .

One surly Clown lookt out, and said,
I'll fling the P—— pot on your head;
You sha'n't come here nor get a Sous
You look like Rogues would rob a House.
                 (1–18, 37–40)

If Baucis and Philemon are humble villagers, they should, Swift implies, act like humble people and, in a contemporization of the tale, live in an ordinary country village and speak in colloquial accents.

Quoth Baucis, this is wholsom Fare,
Eat, Honest Friends, and never spare,
And if we find our Vittels fail
We can but make it out in Ale.
                (63–66)

If they serve a humble meal, it must not run into several courses

of pastoral delicacies. If the hut is turned into a church, the procedure by which its parts and contents are transformed into
their respective counterparts must be given in step-by-step detail. The nature of the travesty of Ovidian convention is suggested
by the specific mention of metamorphosis in lines 147–52:

> A Bed-sted in the antique mode
>
> .   .   .   .
>
> Was Metamorphos't into Pews;
> Which yet their former Virtue keep,
> By lodging Folks dispos'd to sleep.

This emphasis on retention of "their former Virtue" informs
Swift's travesty, with its literal and physical detail. The comic,
even satiric, nature of the metamorphoses is conveyed by lines
153–54—"The Cottage with such Feats as these / Grown to a
Church by just Degrees"—and 161–62—"You've rais'd a Church
here in a Minute, / And I would fain continue in it." It is witty
and good fun, which is surely Swift's main purpose,[18] but there
is also some parody present.

The immediate target of the parody is most likely Dryden,[19]
for Dryden goes well beyond Ovid in romanticizing the humble
poverty of the couple and in detailing the way their lives were
changed. Thus Ovid's "parvo aeno" ["little copper kettle"] (645)
becomes, in Dryden, a vessel shining "like burnish'd Gold" (57);
"ad flammas anima producit anili" ["blowing them into flame
with the breath of her old body"] (643) becomes "with trembling
Breath she blows, / Till in a chearful Blaze the Flames arose"
(52–53); and, though Dryden, in line 30, says the roof of the
"homely Shed" was "not far from Ground," in line 62 a chine of
bacon hangs "High o'er the Hearth." This romanticizing tendency appears most clearly in the account of the meal. What Swift
describes as "wholsom Fare"—slices from a flitch of bacon "tosst
up in a Pan with Batter, / And serv'd up in an earthen Platter"
(58–63)—Dryden labels a "Feast" and glorifies by his choice of
adjectives:

Autumnal Cornels next in order serv'd,
In Lees of Wine well pickl'd, and preserv'd.
A Garden-Sallad was the third Supply,
Of Endive, Radishes, and Succory:
Then Curds and Cream, the Flow'r of Country-Fare,
And new-laid Eggs, which *Baucis* busie Care
Turn'd by a gentle Fire, and roasted rear.

. . . .

The Second Course succeeds like that before,
Plums, Apples, Nuts, and of their Wintry Store,
Dry Figs, and Grapes, and wrinkl'd Dates were set
In Canisters, t' enlarge the little Treat:
All these a Milk-white Honey-comb surround,
Which in the midst the Country-Banquet crown'd.

("Baucis and Philemon," 92–117)

Finally, Dryden concludes his fable with a vivid, detailed, nearly ludicrous example of exactly the sort of physical, literal metamorphosis that Swift's poem abounds in:

Old *Baucis* is by old *Philemon* seen
Sprouting with sudden Leaves of spritely Green:
Old *Baucis* look'd where old *Philemon* stood,
And saw his lengthen'd Arms a sprouting Wood:
New Roots their fasten'd Feet begin to bind,
Their Bodies stiffen in a rising Rind:
Then e'er the Bark above their Shoulders grew,
They give and take at once their last Adieu:
At once, Farewell, O faithful Spouse, they said;
At once th' incroaching Rinds their closing Lips invade.

("Baucis and Philemon," 181–90)

This metamorphosis, in which much of Dryden's detail is not justified by the Ovidian original, is one which Swift omits from his manuscript and passes over very briefly in his printed poem—what could he add to it?

Swift's aims in "The Story of Baucis and Philemon"—of relating well a humorous story and making sport of Dryden's style in translation—were often the aims of later poems as well. As Herbert Davis reminds us, "It has perhaps not been clearly enough recognized that a good number of Swift's pieces owe their existence entirely to such purely literary motives."[20] For a travesty, and for this point in Swift's career, that is purpose enough; for an imitation—the next logical step in handling the classics—more seriousness and depth would be required. Swift went on to this step two years later in "Baucis and Philemon. Imitated, From the Eighth Book of Ovid." Eric Rothstein has analyzed in detail Swift's handling of the imitative form and of the use of allusions in developing it:

Addison seems to have seen, and to have brought Swift to see, that the direction of "Baucis and Philemon" should be determined by the imitation of Ovid through inversion. This mode of inversion . . . is not verbal, or the sort of narrative parody that plays with a sequence of events, but ideological. . . . From this twin tradition [of the Ovidian theme of piety, reinforced by Christian ethics] Swift drew the methods and themes of his imitation: contemporary (Christian) application of the myth; the defining of spiritual identity through material change—disguise, relocation, and metamorphosis; and finally, Providential justice.[21]

Much of the inspiration for the revision was probably Addison's: under his guidance Swift was able to produce a poem of great ingenuity and depth. But the techniques did not become sufficiently a part of Swift for him to be able to follow them up directly, and the natural course of development of the imitation in Swift is, instead, from "The Story of Baucis and Philemon" to the Horatian imitations nearly a decade later.

III ⤙

Before this final step in the handling of the imitation, however, come the allusive techniques of the two "Description" poems. First is the less specific use of an external influence illustrated by "A Description of the Morning," which I will not consider here.

Roger Savage, in a thorough discussion of this poem, shows how Swift drew upon a tradition—perhaps having specific poems in mind as models, perhaps only types—in order to impose on that tradition his own realistic bent: "The poem is basically mock-*descriptio*, a comic imitation of the classical ideal."[22] Although one cannot identify specific works which served as a source for the poem, examples of the type of poem Swift was imitating, which gave the impetus and supplied the ideas to be developed, are cited by Savage.

An earlier example of the same procedure is "Verses Wrote in a Lady's Ivory Table-Book." The poem's date is uncertain; Williams follows Swift in placing it first among his tetrameter poems but has doubts about the early date (1698) Swift assigned it. The date given in Faulkner's edition, 1706, and Deane Swift's date, sometime between 1703 and 1706, support the stylistic evidence that it was not the first of Swift's efforts in tetrameters. Perhaps, as Williams suggests, it was "written early and revised about 1706."[23]

Although no definite source can be identified for the "Verses," a convincing example of the type of poem which was his starting point is William Walsh's "Epigram. Written in a Lady's Table-Book":

> With what strange Raptures wou'd my Soul be blest,
> Were but her Book an Emblem of her Breast?
> As I from that all former Marks efface,
> And, uncontroul'd, put new ones in their place;
> So might I chase all others from her Heart,
> And my own Image in the stead impart.
> But, ah! how short the Bliss wou'd prove, if he
> Who seiz'd it next, might do the same by me.[24]

Swift's poem bears several resemblances to Walsh's, in setting the book as an emblem of its owner and in the ease with which its contents can be erased; and Walsh's poem is, indeed, just the sort of wit which Swift says is scribbled in such a book. Using either that poem or the tradition of poems like it as a starting point, Swift writes his own delightfully comic, but truthful, version.

The casual surface of the "Verses" originates with the prosopopeia, by which the tablebook itself describes and discusses its contents in a coolly derisive tone.

> Peruse my Leaves thro' ev'ry Part,
> And think thou seest my owners Heart,
> Scrawl'd o'er with Trifles thus, and quite
> As hard, as sensless, and as light:
> Expos'd to every Coxcomb's Eyes,
> But hid with Caution from the Wise.
>
> (1–6)

Depth is added as the tablebook becomes a surrogate for its owner (2) and the catalog of notes written in it (7–16) evinces the character of its "owners Heart":

> Here you may read (*Dear Charming Saint*)
> Beneath (*A new Receit for Paint*)
> Here in Beau-spelling (*tru tel deth*)
> There in her own (*far an el breth*)
> Here (*lovely Nymph pronounce my doom*)
> There (*A safe way to use Perfume*)
> Here, a Page fill'd with Billet Doux;
> On t'other side (*laid out for Shoes*)
> (*Madam, I dye without your Grace*)
> (*Item, for half a Yard of Lace*.)

The juxtaposed notes expose two complementary sides of the lady's affected, frivolous life, one side exposed in the scribblings of the beaux and fops, the other side in her own jottings. The fops contribute the internal affectations of romantic love: "*Dear Charming Saint*," "*tru tel deth*," "*lovely Nymph pronounce my doom*," "*Billet Doux*," and "*Madam, I dye without your Grace*." The lady's notes reflect the external affectations of physical appearance, in which paints, breath mints, perfumes, and lace are as much a façade for physical reality as the romantic slogans are for spiritual vacuity. The only contact the list has with reasonable life occurs in line 14—"*laid out for Shoes*"—which sets off the other items but also discloses the level of the lady's thoughts when she does turn to the real world. Lines 9 and 10 are especially indicative of the world the poem is attacking, as the inaccurate spellings symbolize its falsity. The "Beau-spelling" ("*tru tel deth*") purposely distorts the truth in order to gain an effect and to create its own world with its own manners and mores. The lady's spelling ("*far an el breth*") suggests an unconscious ignorance of the truth, both of the conventions of spelling and of the worthwhile values of life. The alternations make the internal and the external, the spiritual (e.g., "*Saint*," "*Grace*") and the material ("*Paint*," "*Lace*"), completely interchangeable and equate the significant with the insignificant in this artificial world.

The satire on the world of fashionable ladies and gentlemen, with the implication that their lives, like those in *The Rape of the Lock*, are encompassed entirely by cosmetics, cards, and courtships, is extended in the final six lines:

> Whoe're expects to hold his part
> In such a Book and such a Heart,
> If he be Wealthy and a Fool
> Is in all Points the fittest Tool,
> Of whom it may be justly said,
> He's a Gold Pencil tipt with Lead.
> (25–30)

These lines nicely round out and unify the poem, returning to the identification of owner with book in line 26 and, through the multiple meanings of lines 28 and 30, reemphasizing the main satiric themes of the earlier portion. On the literal level a pencil to be used by the lady corresponds wittily to the basic metaphor of the tablebook. And on the figurative level, that the "Gold Pencil" is "tipt with Lead"—a metal symbolic of worthlessness and stupidity—extends the dominant thematic motifs of affectation and appearance. The lady's concern with physical appear-

ance turns into the desire for wealth conveyed by the literal
meanings of "Wealthy" and "Gold," while the man's ethereal
romanticizings are un   cut by the figurative implications of
"Tool" and "Lead   e juxtaposition of "Gold" and "Lead," in
a "Tool" to ca   he lady's wishes, places a final judgment
upon the valu   ociety which the lady and her gentlemen
represent.

But the satii   ionable society is not left there, as an
abstract satire   lass life in the late seventeenth or early
eighteenth cen   , Lines 17-24 turn the satire outward, toward
the reader:

> Who that had Wit would place it here,
> For every peeping Fop to Jear.
> To think that your Brains Issue is
> Expos'd to th' Excrement of his,
> In power of Spittle and a Clout
> When e're he please to blot it out;
> And then to heighten the Disgrace
> Clap his own Nonsence in the place.

Although the tablebook is the speaker of the lines "Who that
had Wit would place it here, / For every peeping Fop to Jear,"
the title focuses attent   on the person who wrote these verses
in a lady's ivory table   The poet himself has wit but "placed
it" in the book, wh   to s can jeer and blot it out. That, however, is a risk the sa   t always takes His wisdom is always exposed to the excrement of the "chatt'ring throng" ("To Mr.
Congreve," 223) he is attacking; his wisdom can be "blotted
out" by any reader who chooses to jeer at it, rather than learn
from it. And that is precisely the point. Anybody who secretly
yearns for the sterile life the lady and her beaux lead, who allows his or her standards and values to become even partially
identified with theirs, who confuses their appearances and triv-
ialities with truth and reality, is one with the fops who blot out
wit and then scrawl nonsense in ladies' ivory tablebooks.

IV

Of the early poems, "A Description of a City Shower" moves closest in its use of allusions to poems later in Swift's career. Here Swift follows a specific work, rather than a type, drawing from it for tone and structure. Although he not yet imitate his model in a sustained way or use its allusions to expand and deepen his theme, in vivid detail and subtlety his poem is the finest of the early verse satires.

Irvin Ehrenpreis has pointed out the use of Virgil's first *Georgic*, 322–92, as the model for the poem's threefold division into omens, preliminaries, and deluge.[25] Here, for the first time, Swift constructs a matrix of allusions which lends a structure to his poem and allows him to devote his energies to details. As Swift develops the details, however, he does not use the main source to shape or strengthen his theme, as he will later in his career. The allusions in the poem are to Dryden's translations rather than to Virgil himself, and they draw Dryden's words, rather than their Virgilian contexts, into the poem.[26] Ehrenpreis mentions several lines in the poem which would have reminded readers of Dryden: "Here rious Kinds by various Fortunes led" (39), for example, rec Dryden's line "On various Seas, by various Tempests tost' (*Aeneid*, I, 320, 519, and elsewhere). Ehrenpreis also suggests that Dryden's translation of the simile in the *Aeneid*, VII, 528–3 (the first except below), resembles, in tone, structure, and specific details, Swift's simile in 17–22:

> And, as young Striplings whip the Top for sport,
> On the smooth Pavement of an empty Court;
> The wooden Engine flies and whirls about,
> Admir'd, with Clamours, of the Beardless rout;
> They lash aloud, each other they provoke,
> And lend their little Souls at ev'ry stroke.

> Brisk *Susan* whips her Linen from the Rope,
> While the first drizzling Show'r is born aslope,

> Such is that Sprinkling which some careless Quean
> Flirts on you from her Mop, but not so clean.
> You fly, invoke the Gods; then turning, stop
> To rail; she singing, still whirls on her Mop.

There are other close echoes of Dryden. Swift's line "A coming
Show'r your shooting Corns presage, / Old Aches throb, your
hollow Tooth will rage" (9–10) parallels these lines in the first
Georgic: "And that by certain signs we may presage / Of Heats
and Rains, and Wind's impetuous rage" (483–84). And Swift's
"Not yet, the Dust had shun'd th' unequal Strife" (23) is very
close to Dryden's "Amaz'd, he wou'd have shun'd th' unequal
Fight" (*Aeneid*, II, 508).

These allusions, like the echoing of Garth's *Dispensary*, first
glossed by Faulkner, are witty. Invoking familiar passages from
Dryden's well-known translations, they create agreeable and
sometimes amusing recollections in the readers' minds and reinforce the generally light tone. That tone and the quality of the
allusions militate against a serious or didactic interpretation of
the poem.[27] That the allusions, together with the concluding
triplet, focus primarily on Dryden rather than on Virgil confirms the lightness of the poem's theme. Swift himself, in a letter
to Thomas Beach in 1735, pointed to the satire on Dryden's use
of triplets and alexandrines: "I was so angry at these corruptions, that above twenty-four years ago I banished them all by
one triplet, with the Alexandrine, upon a very ridiculous subject" (*Corres.*, IV, 321). Swift's own words emphasize the humor
of the poem and suggest that in it, as in "The Story of Baucis
and Philemon," he was having fun at the expense of the poet
who turned Virgil's gold into "rusty Iron" (*The Battle of the Books*,
p. 247).

Through allusions, then, Swift twits Dryden; but also through
allusions he achieves some of the best humorous and satiric
effects of the poem. The first is the allusion to the biblical flood:
"Now in contiguous Drops the Flood comes down, / Threat'ning

with Deluge this *Devoted* Town" (31–32). The allusion involves
a double hyperbole—the absurdities of expecting a shower to
cause a deluge and thinking the wickedness even of "this *Devoted*
[*OED*: 'doomed'] Town" comparable to the evil in Noah's day.
The evil of the town, however, is not the utter corruption and
violence God beheld in Noah's day, but, at least according to
Swift's account, a series of very human vanities and hypocrisies:

> To Shops in Crouds the dagged Females fly,
> Pretend to cheapen Goods, but nothing buy.
> The Templer spruce, while ev'ry Spout's a-broach,
> Stays till 'tis fair, yet seems to call a Coach.
> (33–36)

The poem is a celebration rather than a condemnation of city
life: there is full appreciation of the richness and diversity of the
city as well as tolerant recognition of its faults. The wit and exaggeration in these allusions supply the context and perspective
for the "realism" of the concluding section:

> Now from all Parts the swelling Kennels flow,
> And bear their Trophies with them as they go:
>
> .   .   .   .
>
> Sweepings from Butchers Stalls, Dung, Guts, and Blood,
> Drown'd Puppies, stinking Sprats, all drench'd in Mud,
> Dead Cats and Turnip-Tops come tumbling down the Flood.
> (53–54, 61–63)

The threatened "Deluge," then, turns out to be a gutter-flusher,
itself described through an allusion. Ehrenpreis has pointed out
that the final line of the poem echoes a line from Dryden's translation of the *Georgics*: "And cakes of rustling Ice come rolling
down the Flood" (I, 418).[28] The allusion tempers the "realistic"
effect of the details and supplements the light, witty tone which
makes this the best of the early satires in verse.

Among those caught in the city shower, an intriguing figure is
the poet:

Ah! where must needy Poet seek for Aid,
When Dust and Rain at once his Coat invade;
His only Coat, where Dust confus'd with Rain,
Roughen the Nap, and leave a mingled Stain.
                                    (27–30)

Swift, coincidentally or not, showed a similar concern about the effect of a sudden shower on his clothes: "It has been a terrible rainy day, but so flattering in the morning, that I would needs go out in my new hat" (*Journal to Stella*, II, 396). Whether or not the lines in the poem depict Swift literally, they do suggest figuratively his literary dilemma in the first decade of the eighteenth century: where does a poet in need of aid seek help? For Swift, at least, the answer was tetrameters and allusions. By the end of 1710 they have established the form and manner Swift's verse will have for the rest of his career. The early dullness of the tetrameter couplets turns, during that decade, into a witty, rapid colloquial style; and early problems with structure and unity have begun to be solved, by the end of the decade, through the use of allusions. There remain only to sharpen these techniques by experience and, through that experience, to learn how to express more fully the truth Swift regarded as essential in poetry.

III

Thoughts Borrowed from Virgil and Horace
The Early Personal Poems

When Swift returned to the classical imitation in 1712, some seven years after "The Description of a Salamander," it was to begin a series of Horatian imitations. These are important, first, because they show Swift moving to a more inclusive use of allusion than the echoing of phrases, as in the odes, or the supplying of a framework for an otherwise independent poem, as in the early satires. Swift begins now to use classical works as models for tone and theme as well as for structure and, by integrating all of these with his previously established style, to fashion works of greater depth and complexity than he had previously created. And they are important, second, because they enabled Swift to reach a deeper level of truth in his poems: not just the vague abstractions of the odes, or the constricted realism of the early satires, but a fuller knowledge of life and people that comes through experience and reflection. This broader use of allusion—

61

to unify structure, tone, and theme into a significant apprehension and expression of truth—develops in the early imitations of Horace and gives depth and strength to Swift's first great poem on himself, "Cadenus and Vanessa."

I

Two of the four Horatian imitations written between 1712 and 1714 are political poems which use Horace in a fairly straightforward, unsubtle way to attack Lord Nottingham and Richard Steele. The earliest, "T—l——d's Invitation to Dismal, to Dine with the Calves-Head Club" (1712), an imitation of the fifth epistle of the first book, turns Horace's good-humored dinner invitation into a fierce indictment of regicide, profaneness, and infidelity. The opening of Swift's poem—which transforms Horace's "holus omne" ["a dinner of herbs only"],[1] with its wholesomeness and pastoral simplicity, into the "single Dish" (2) symbolic of Charles I—uses Horace to establish the standard of values against which everything in the poem must be measured. Horace made a point of associating his dinner with "cras nato Caesare festus" ["the festal day of Caesar's birth"], with its religious and patriotic overtones: "Two Years after [Caesar's] Death the Triumvirs ordered, that his Birth-day should be celebrated by the People crowned with Laurel, and that whoever neglected it should be devoted to the Vengeance of Jupiter, and the deceased God himself."[2] In contrast to Horace's poem, celebrating Caesar's birthday, Swift dates his poem January 29, the eve of Charles's death-day. In doing so, Swift uses in passing a well-established parallel between Charles and Caesar. The parallel honors Charles by association with a great classical figure, one who was assassinated by those who regarded him as a tyrant and whose death set in motion a great civil conflict. The anniversary of Charles's death also had religious significance, having been designated by Parliament "for ever hereafter set apart to be kept and observed in all the Churches and Chapels of your Majesties Kingdoms . . . as an Anniversary day of Fasting and Humiliation."[3] The weight of both these days, with their dual emphasis on piety and patriotism, is brought to bear against the impiety and treachery of the club.

The central theme in the opening lines of Swift's poem, those describing the dinner, is impiety. The word Horace uses for the meal to which he is inviting Torquatus has religious overtones: Lewis and Short give "a vessel used in sacrifice, an offering dish" as a second meaning for *patella*. Swift uses this detail, elaborating on it and turning it ironically into a mock-Mass to which the well-known freethinker John Toland invites Lord Nottingham:

> To morrow We our *Mystick Feast* prepare,
> Where Thou, our latest *Proselyte*, shalt share:
> When We, by proper Signs and Symbols tell,
> How, by *Brave Hands*, the *Royal TRAYTOR* fell;
> The Meat shall represent the *TYRANT*'s Head,
> The Wine, his Blood, *our Predecessors* shed:
> Whilst an *alluding* Hymn some Artist sings,
> We toast Confusion to the Race of Kings.
>
> (7–14)

The religious rites were indeed a part of the festivities, according to *The secret History of the Calves-Head Club; or, The Republican Unmasked. Wherein is fully shewn the Religion of the Calves-Head Heroes, in their Anniversary Thanksgiving-Songs on the Thirtieth of January* (1703):

By another gentleman . . . I was informed, . . . that the company wholly consisted of Independents and Anabaptists . . . ; that the famous Jerry White, formerly chaplain to Oliver Cromwell . . . said grace; that, after the table-cloth was removed, the Anniversary Anthem, as they impiously called it, was sung, and a calf's skull, filled with wine or other liquor; and then a brimmer went about to the pious memory of those worthy patriots that had killed the tyrant, and delivered their country from his arbitrary sway.[4]

There is sacrilege in this, and a basic abuse of history. Horace's "sermone benigno" emphasizes the good old days (if one accepts Dacier's reading "archaicis lectis"[5]), affirming the values and virtues of the past. In Swift's poem the club's appeal for treason uses, rather than affirms, the past, making past evils a model for present and future conduct.

Swift's target, however, is not some small, secretive, and possibly mythical club,[6] but the entire Whig faction. In the following verse paragraph he turns Horace's "panegyric upon Wine, short, but spirited,"[7] into a forceful attack on Whig leaders:

> Who, by Disgraces or ill Fortune sunk,
> Feels not his Soul enliven'd when he's Drunk?
> Wine can clear up *Godolphin's* cloudy Face,
> And fill *Jack Smith* with Hopes to keep his Place;
> By Force of Wine ev'n *Scarborough* is Brave,
> *Hal Boyle* grows more Pert, and *Sommers* not so Grave:
> Wine can give *Portland* Wit, and *Cleveland* Sense,
> *Montague* Learning, *Bolton* Eloquence.
> (17–24; contractions expanded)

What was in Horace a quiet meeting of a small, select group of friends becomes in Swift's poem a noisy gathering of persons with only their political interests in common. By making the club inclusive rather than exclusive, Swift attributes the impiety and treason described in the opening verse paragraph to all Whigs and extends into verse a campaign he had been carrying on in *The Examiner*, where he had charged that the Whigs have "a Design of destroying the *Established Church*" and are "Enemies to Monarchy": "The Regard they bear to our *Monarchy*, hath appeared by their open ridiculing the *Martyrdom* of King *Charles* the First, in their *Calves-head Clubs*, their common Discourses and their Pamphlets."[8] Swift's main concern in 1712, however, was not the ridicule of Charles I, but the implications the situation of the 1640s, with its strife over rulers and religion, held for the contemporary situation. The death of Charles becomes symbolic of Whig opposition to the Queen and her ministry. Such opposition was illustrated dramatically several weeks before publication of "Toland's Invitation," when Bishop Fleetwood published four old sermons together with a new preface undercutting Queen Anne indirectly by effusive praise of William and Mary and directly by limiting its endorsement to the first seven years of her reign (1702–9, those of the Whig ministry). It also accused the Tory ministry, quite pointedly, of favoring the Pretender: "I have lived to see our Deliverance from *Arbitrary Power* and *Popery*, traduced and vilify'd by some, who, formerly, thought it was their greatest Merit, . . . and others who, without it, must have lived in Exile, Poverty, and Misery, meanly disclaiming it, and using ill the *glorious Instrument* thereof."[9] At a time when charges of Jacobitism were in the air and the question of the Protestant succession seemed still to be unresolved, Horace's poem, with its emphasis on piety and patriotism, provided a meaningful vehicle for Swift's attack on Whig attitudes which, in the words of the Tory House of Commons, were "malicious and factious, . . . tending to create Discord and Sedition amongst her [Majesty's] Subjects."[10]

At the heart of Horace's epistle is friendship, the "conviva" among "fidos . . . amicos" (1, 24). Swift makes this theme the unifying motif of his imitation. He refers ironically in line 4, for example, to "your trusty Friends"; can men guilty of treason, men celebrating the assassination of a monarch, men opposed to the government and church, possess trust, that indispensable prerequisite to friendship? Dismal, on the contrary, exemplifies the untrustworthiness Swift wants to associate with all Whigs: "Lord Nottingham, a famous Tory and speech-maker, is gone over to the Whig side: they toast him daily, and Lord Wharton says, It is *Dismal* (so they call him from his looks) will save England at last."[11] The price the Whigs paid for Nottingham's opposition to the peace was supporting his bill to prohibit Occasional Conformity, thus voting against their stated principles and against their dissenting supporters: "I did indeed see a Letter at that time from One of them to a Great Man [Harley], complaining that they were betrayed, and undone by their pretended Friends."[12] Are not all Whigs, then, like Dismal, men with "vain ambitious Hopes" (5), men always "hunting after Bribes" (6)? There is a similar irony about the word *love* in lines 31–32 ("You shall be . . . / Seated at Table next the Men you love"). Can men both "love" and praise regicide? The contrast of a later line with its classical counterpart brings out the paradox: in Horace, Sabinus will come "nisi cena prior potiorque puella . . . detinet" ["unless a better supper and a goodlier girl detain him"]. As Dacier points out, the tone of Horace's lines assures that the suggestion must be taken tongue-in-cheek, for Horace would not consider seriously the possibility that his friends might choose some casual, superficial relationship over the deeper, more lasting joys of friendship. There is no such playfulness in the equivalent lines of Swift's poem. The light love suggested in Horace changes to lust, and the irony turns into exposure of the "lover's" character:

> Wh[arto]n, unless prevented by a Whore,
> Will hardly fail.
> (35–36)

The Whigs' questionable personal loyalties reflect on their national loyalties, and both contrast to the personal and political fidelity which permeates Horace's poem.

In the *Journal to Stella* Swift asks Stella and Rebecca, "Have you seen Toland's Invitation to Dismal;? How do you like it? but it is an Imitation of Horace, and perhaps you don't understand Horace" (II, 544). An awareness of the Horatian original is not in fact essential to understanding the poem, but it does enable one to appreciate more fully how Swift, by playing his poem off against a complimentary, good-humored invitation to a meal with friends, achieves a witty but intense attack not just on Nottingham but on the principles and morals of Whigs in general.

In the other political imitation, "The First Ode of the Second

Book of Horace Paraphras'd: And Address'd to *Richard St——le,*
Esq." (1714), the imitation becomes more complex and detailed.
The basic technique is still ironic reversal, as Swift uses similarities to and differences from Horace to reinforce his attacks on
Steele. The central departure from Horace, of course, involves
the addressee. Horace wrote to Pollio, renowned as a warrior,
tragedian, and patriot, and at the time, writing a history of the
civil wars.[13] Steele is made to appear inconsequential by contrast
with this noble standard. Swift opens with nine lines of mock-
praise of Steele which do not have a parallel in Horace:

> *Dick*, thour't resolv'd, as I am told,
> Some strange *Arcana* to unfold,
> And with the help of *Buckley*'s Pen
> To vamp the *good Old Cause* again,
> Which thou (such *Bur——t*'s shrewd Advice is)
> Must furbish up and Nickname *CRISIS.*
>
> (1–6)

In his translation of Horace, however, Thomas Creech supplies
an introductory stanza, apparently not needed in Horace's day,
which sets off Swift's opening nicely:

> Sad Prisoners Guard, and Glory of the Bar
> The Senate's Oracle, and great in War,
> Whose faith and Vertue all proclaim;
> To whom the *German* Triumph won
> Eternal Fame,
> And never fading Glories of a Crown.[14]

The appropriateness of comparing Steele to Pollio, and the effect of the comparison, comes out in a series of undercutting
parallels. Pollio's noble undertaking is "periculosae plenum . . .
aleae" ["full of dangerous hazard"][15]; Steele's, in contrast, "May
bring in Jeopardy thy Bacon" (30). Pollio is known for his
"severae Musa tragoediae" ["stern tragic muse"]; Steele writes
farce and wicked verse. Pollio is "insigne maestis praesidium
reis" ["a famed support of anxious clients"]; Steele is a "Friend
to [such] Distress'd" as

> buxom Lasses [repenting]
> Their luckless Choice of Husbands—others,
> Impatient to be like their Mothers.
> (52–54)

Pollio is "consulenti . . . curiae" ["bulwark of the Senate in its councils"]; Steele, newly elected member for Stockbridge, will make the Senate "feel thy Eloquence and Fire, / Approve thy Schemes, thy Wit admire" (61–62). Swift uses Horace, then, to shape and control his attack on Steele, but also to strengthen it: the series of parallels to Pollio provides a constant reminder of how poorly Steele's accomplishments measure up against a standard of ancient and acknowledged worth.

Swift also uses Horace's main theme—peace—to undermine Steele. Horace's poem supports Pollio's efforts to expose the causes and effects of the civil wars and comments on the devastating effect of civil wars on Rome. In a key contrast Swift juxtaposes Pollio's study of the "belli . . . causas" ["causes of the war"] to Steele's railings "at the *Peace*, / And all its secret *Causes*" (15–16). Thus Swift expands his theme beyond personal attack and strikes a blow for the Tory side:

An impartial Historian may tell the World (and the next Age will easily believe what it continues to feel) that the Avarice and Ambition of a few factious insolent Subjects, had almost destroyed their Country, by continuing a ruinous War, in Conjunction with Allies, for whose Sakes principally we fought, who refused to bear their just Proportion of the Charge, and were connived at in their Refusal for private Ends.[16]

In contrast to Rome's "gravis . . . / principum amicitias" ["friendships of leaders that boded ill"] are Steele's tales "of *Leagues* among the Great / Portending ruin to our State" (21–22). And in contrast to Horace's "arma / nondum expiatis uncta cruoribus" ["weapons stained with blood as yet unexpiated"] stands Steele's grievance,

> The Q——n (*forsooth, Despotick*) gave
> Twelve *Coronets*, without *thy* leave!
> A Breach of Liberty, 'tis own'd,

For which no Heads have *yet* atton'd!
(25–28)

Horace's theme reaches its climax in two magnificent stanzas on the "melancholy Effects of the whole civil War."[17]

> quis non Latino sanguine pinguior
> campus sepulcris impia proelia
>   testatur auditumque Medis
>   Hesperiae sonitum ruinae?
>
> qui gurges aut quae flumina lugubris
> ignara belli? quod mare Dauniae
>   non decoloravere caedes?
>   quae caret ora cruore nostro?

[What plain is not enriched with Latin blood, to bear witness with its graves to our unholy strife and to the sound of Hesperia's fall, heard even by the Medes! What pool or stream has failed to taste the dismal war! What sea has Italian slaughter not discoloured! What coast knows not our blood!]

The contrasting tone supports the choice of details as Swift ridicules Steele's concerns:

> Now manfully thou'lt run a Tilt
> "On *Popes*, for all the Blood they've spilt,
> "For Massacres, and Racks, and Flames,
> "For Lands enrich'd by crimson Streams,
> "For Inquisitions taught by *Spain*,
> "Of which the Christian World complain.
> (93–98)

In "The Publick Spirit of the Whigs," Swift with difficulty and at length "remarked upon the Falshoods and Absurdities" of Steele's pamphlet *The Crisis* (*Prose Works*, VIII, 66). The poem accomplishes the same purpose, but with a welcome brevity and infinitely greater wit.

The increased complexity of Swift's imitative technique, the movement toward union of poem and source, is shown by some witty and satiric verbal interplay with Horace. The lines on the "*Bucket-play* 'twixt Whigs and Tories, / Their ups and downs" (17–18) which Steele describes in his writings, although witty in themselves, are enriched by juxtaposition with their counterpart, the "ludum . . . Fortunae" ["game of Fortune"] which Pollio will describe. Horace, to stress the gravity of his undertaking and the danger he risks from it, writes to Pollio, "incedis per ignes / suppositos cineri doloso" ["thou art walking, as it were, over fires hidden beneath treacherous ashes"]; comparison with that line reveals the wit in Swift's corresponding advice to Steele that "Since [he has] got into the Fire" (33), he had better continue party writing until he gets all such nonsense out of his system. When Swift urges Steele's return to drama after he has "settled *Europe*'s *Grand* Affairs" (40), the language reflects the "grande munus" ["lofty calling"] ascribed to Pollio at the same point; and Horace's line "duces, / non indecoro pulvere sordidos" ["captains begrimed with no inglorious dust"] shaped the truly inglorious "*black-guard Rout*" (79) which shouts acclaim of Steele in Swift's poem. And when Swift urges Steele to give up this writing, so "foreign to thy Walk" (102), and join him in retiring "To some snug Cellar" to write tender sonnets to "our *Dolls* and *Jenneys*" (109, 116), there is a humorous echo of Horace's intent to retire with his Muse "Dionaeo sub antro" ["in the shadow of some Dionean grotto"]. With wit and even humor Swift derides the character, thought, and works of Richard Steele by associating him ironically with the sincere praise, serious theme, and noble diction of Horace's ode to Pollio.

In these poems, then, Horace is not just the source of a witty idea, as Pliny was for "The Description of a Salamander." Swift, finding a Horatian poem whose topic and themes can be made to fit the situation at hand, assimilates that poem into his own. Horace's poem provides a structure for Swift's work and a value system against which the reader is forced to judge the principles and actions of Steele, Nottingham, and the Whigs in general. In fact, Horace's poem literally becomes a part of Swift's poem, printed at the foot of the page, and necessary for full understanding and appreciation of the meaning and wit of the poem. It was only as Swift turned the Horatian imitations upon himself, however, that he was able to go significantly beyond ironic reversals to a combination of poem and allusions which would enable him to explore new ranges of experience and communicate deeper levels of truth. In the simple inversions of the political poems, Swift uses the imitation to reinforce readily apparent truths by contrasting examples from antiquity. In the poems on himself, Swift uses the imitation to conceal or obscure truths which become apparent only after close comparison with the Horatian models. Through the imitation Swift is able to write on topics too close and delicate to be treated in any other way and to explore such personal areas more deeply than he had before.

In the earlier of the two poems on himself, "Part of the Seventh Epistle of the First Book of Horace Imitated" (1713), Swift accomplishes his purposes by a subtle interplay between his characters and those of Horace. Swift introduces the characters in his poem—Harley and himself—by favorable comparisons to the corresponding characters in Horace's poem. The imitation, first, provides indirect support for Swift's direct praise of Harley. The opening lines associate Harley with the "strenuus et fortis" ["vigour and courage"] of Lucius Marcus Philippus, who was, according to the commentators, "equally distinguished by his Birth, Eloquence, and Courage, which raised him to the Censorship and Consulship."[18] The paralleling of Philippus and Harley enables Swift to give more graciously, because less overtly, and more effectively, because of the added compliment by association, the sort of praise he was also willing to give directly: "I shall take the liberty of thinking and calling You, the ablest and faithfullest Minister, and truest Lover of Your Country that this Age hath produced."[19] But the imitation also, and less obviously, provides the basis for Swift to write about himself. Swift can "justify" and give objectivity to the descriptions of himself by implying that he is simply following details supplied by his original. That is not, in fact, the case at all: Horace's lines describing Vulteius Mena are much shorter and less specific than Swift's sections on himself. In the first of these, Swift gives eight lines (5–12) to a topic Horace handled in two and a half. In the other, Swift expands two lines on Vulteius to twenty lines on himself:

> tenui censu, sine crimine, notum
> et properare loco et cessare et quaerere et uti.

[Of modest fortune and blameless record, known to work hard and idle in season, to make money and spend it.]

> A Clergyman of special Note,
> For shunning those of his own Coat;
> Which made his Brethren of the Gown
> Take care betimes to run him down:
> No Libertine, nor Over-nice,
> Addicted to no sort of Vice;
> Went where he pleas'd, said what he thought,
> Not Rich, but ow'd no Man a Groat;
> In State-Opinions, *a-la Mode*,
> He hated *Wh[arto]n* like a Toad;
> Had giv'n the *Faction* many a Wound,
> And Libell'd all the *Junta* round;
> Kept Company with Men of Wit,
> Who often father'd what he writ;
> His Works were hawk'd in ev'ry Street,
> But seldom rose above a Sheet:
> Of late indeed the Paper-*Stamp*
> Did very much his Genius cramp;
> And, since he could not spend his Fire,
> He now intended to Retire.
>   (27–46)

The passages are of interest because, despite the seemingly objective tone created by the third-person pronouns and the use of Horace as "source," they describe Swift as he wanted to be seen.

And they are important because they supply the foundation for his defense of himself and for his theme in the poem.

At the same time that Swift suggests his characters are like their counterparts in Horace, he also brings out important differences, and through these—signaled by the handling of time in the second portrait—he achieves his purposes in the poem. Swift unobtrusively but pointedly combines events between 1710 and 1713 into a fictional present. At the time he met Harley in 1710, for example, Swift did not yet hate Wharton like a toad and had not yet "libell'd all the *Junta* round." By implying so, however, he gives a sense of uniformity to his political views and obscures the fact that joining Harley meant a change in party affiliation. In 1710 he had no urge to retire from London and seek again the quiet and content of the country—even in 1714 it is more an affectation and a defense than a deep desire. But by claiming, and perhaps believing, that he was ready even in 1710 to leave London, he protects himself from disappointment: he had no ambitions to rise in church or government; he was satisfied with his humble place; he had no desire to be a dean—a canon at Windsor, perhaps, but nothing higher. And in 1710 the Stamp Duty had not yet been passed and Swift's works were not being "hawk'd in ev'ry Street" (41). But the implications that in 1710 he had written a great deal, was staunchly anti-Whig, and was about to leave London are important parts of the strategy of the poem. The contrast between Vulteius Mena in the parent poem, who, though an agreeable companion and honest tradesman, was patronized by Philippus upon a whim, and Swift, who was approached by Harley because he had a great deal to offer the ministry, is central to Swift's purpose and theme.

Horace put his emphasis on Philippus's humor: Philippus happened to see Vulteius, was intrigued by him, found him a unique companion, and thought it would be interesting and amusing to give him the country villa he desired. In line with this, Horace's poem is a warning to others not to fall victim to grand ambitions, to turn from them before it is too late. The theme, growing out of Horace's personal experiences recounted in the early part of the poem, is stated directly in the closing lines:

Qui semel aspexit, quantum dimissa petitis
praestent, mature redeat repetatque relicta.
metiri se quemque suo modulo ac pede verum est.

[Let him, who once has seen how far what he has given up excels what he has sought, go back in time and seek again the things he has left. 'Tis right that each should measure himself by his own rule and standard.]

Swift retains and even expands the emphasis on the patron's humor: Harley, who "Loves Mischief better than his Meat, / Was now dispos'd to crack a Jest" (14–15) by inviting Swift to dinner. Later, "MY LORD wou'd carry on the Jest" by taking Swift to Windsor (81–82). But the effect is different because of the telescoping of time. The talk of jesting contrasts to Harley's actual motive in cultivating Swift's acquaintance, mocks the service Swift performed for the ministry, and puts into perspective the reward he received. By changing the background and tone of the jesting and by omitting the opening section and the concluding lines of Horace's poem, Swift shifts the emphasis from the victim to the patron. Horace stressed each individual's responsibility to keep his ambitions and expectations within proper limits; Swift stresses the responsibility of a patron toward those he has encouraged and aided. Swift had written lightly, but seriously, upon this topic as he returned to Ireland from London several years before.

I must take leave to reproach Your Lordship for a most inhuman piece of Cruelty; for I can call Your extreme good Usage of me no better, since it has taught me to hate the Place where I am banished, and raised my Thoughts to an Imagination, that I might live to be some way usefull or entertaining, if I were permitted to live in Town. . . . You remember very well, My Lord, how another Person of Quality in Horace's time, used to serve a sort of Fellows who had disoblidged him; how he sent them fine Cloaths, and money, which raised their Thoughts and their Hopes, till those were worn out and spent; and then they were ten times more miserable than before.[20]

The reference to a story very like the one in the Seventh Epistle, in a very similar situation and in much the same tone, confirms Swift's purpose in the imitation: the central message, partially hidden by Horace's differing tone and theme, is that since Harley, at his own initiative, brought Swift to the highest levels of social and political life, led Swift to expect much and others to expect much for him, he has a responsibility to provide for him in a way commensurate with his abilities, dignity, and new expectations.

It is with this in mind that Swift describes so vividly the embarrassments and expenses connected with his deanship, all to emphasize the inadequacy of the provision made for him:

> Suppose him gone through all Vexations,
> Patents, Instalments, Abjurations,
> First-Fruits and Tenths, and Chapter-Treats,
> Dues, Payments, Fees, Demands and Cheats.
>
> (101-4)

Thus also, it is very effective that Swift treats his appointment as a joke: "But you resolv'd to have your Jest, / And 'twas a Folly to Contest" (135-36). As with the earlier reference to jests, which linked them with failure to acknowledge Swift's value and Harley's indebtedness, the word here has a sting to it, for in each case it suggests ironically the serious responsibility Harley has not faced up to. The paradoxical final lines—"Then since you now have done your worst, / Pray leave me where you found me. first" (137-38)—are also played off Horace's lines. Horace's conclusion urges a reversal and return before it is too late; Swift omits that qualification and, by asking the impossible of Harley (virginity cannot be restored, to invoke the second meaning in line 137), gives a final emphasis to what is possible: a better position or at least payment of the funds Swift needs to be able to conduct himself fittingly in the position he has. Viewed in one way, then, the poem is deadly serious, almost a frantic plea for assistance. But Swift conceals his theme behind the Horatian model, so that its emphasis on the dupe almost obscures his deeper concern; and he tells the tale with such verve and good humor that the painful tones can be overlooked. The affirmation of Swift's dignity, worth, and independence is blended so nicely with humorous self-satire (especially in lines 59–70) that the depth of emotion behind it can be ignored entirely. The discovery not only that anger and dislike can be controlled and transformed by imitation, but also that deep personal emotions can be distanced and directed, taught Swift a great deal about the value of allusion in poetry, a lesson which bears its first and possibly greatest fruit in "Cadenus and Vanessa."

According to Harold Williams, Swift's other early poem on himself—the imitation of the sixth satire of the second book (1714)—originally ran to 104 lines, with twenty lines following line 8 and the final four couplets added later, at different times (*Poems*, I, 197). The closing lines were a good addition artistically, for they give the poem a neat, symmetrical form,[21] but they cloud Swift's original intent in the poem. The theme of the poem as first conceived was not, as some critics have implied, retirement: "Swift had done the part that pleased him most, the part of Horace, describing the blessings of the country (it was written at Letcombe, remember) and contrasting them to the disquiet of the city and the Court."[22] The added lines do indeed follow Horace in expressing relief at being "Remov'd from all th' ambitious Scene," especially in the final eight lines:

> Thus in a Sea of Folly tost,
> My choicest Hours of Life are lost;
> Yet always wishing to retreat;
> Oh, could I see my Country Seat.
> There leaning near a gentle Brook,
> Sleep, or peruse some antient Book;
> And there in sweet Oblivion drown
> Those Cares that haunt the Court and Town.

But these lines, possibly added by Pope,[23] conflict with the opening lines of the poem, which emphasize not retirement but security, a subtle but important variation on "hoc erat in votis: modus agri non ita magnus" ["this is what I prayed for!—a piece of land not so very large"].

> I often wish'd, that I had clear
> For Life, six hundred Pounds a Year,
> A handsome House to lodge a Friend,
> A River at my Garden's End,
> A Terras Walk, and half a Rood
> Of Land set out to plant a Wood.
>   (1–6)

Swift's earlier imitation had stressed the ministry's (or Harley's) obligation to provide suitably for him after raising his status and expectations. These lines offer a reminder of that, made subtle and almost hidden by being placed opposite the context of Horace's perfect contentment with what he has.

Whether the twenty lines added for the 1738 edition, which follow Horace in expressing satisfaction with "Just what you gave me, Competence," were by Swift or not,[24] they were not a part of Swift's original intention in the poem. The lines which originally followed 1–6 reminded the ministry of the place in England he really should have received:

> Well, now I have all this and more,
> I ask not to increase my Store,
> But should be perfectly content,
> Could I but live on this side *Trent*.
>   (7–10)

Nor do the lines eulogize retirement, as Horace's do. The lines following indicate that Swift expects to spend less than half his time enjoying his house, garden, terras walk, and wood:

> Nor cross the *Channel* twice a Year,
> To spend six Months with *Statesmen* here.
>   (11–12)

The lines, carefully ambiguous, do not say that he would no longer care to spend six months a year with statesmen; a more likely reading is that he would not have to make the dangerous and expensive channel crossing in order to do so. The "handsome House" may be desirable as a retreat, but Swift intends to use it as a retreat from a continued life of service and activity. There is in Swift, now and later, very little of Horace's intense longing for country life as Reuben A. Brower summarizes it: "Reading, sleep, and idleness, and a return to the simple patriarchal society of the Italian farmer-proprietor."[25] The next verse paragraph points out the convenience of a closer location and reminds the ministry of its promised financial assistance:

> I must by all means come to Town,
> 'Tis for the Service of the Crown.
> "*Lewis*; the *Dean* will be of Use,
> "Send for him up, take no Excuse.
> The Toil, the Danger of the Seas;
> Great Ministers ne'er think of these;
> Or let it cost Five hundred Pound,
> No matter where the Money's found;
> It is but so much more in Debt,
> And that they ne'er consider'd yet.
>   (13–22)

The imitation of Horace's retirement theme, then, comes from additions written or urged by others: Pope's added fable of the country and city mice, the twenty-line addition after line 8, and lines 105–12. Swift's own emphasis was quite different, advancing his case to the ministry in the first twenty-two lines and presenting an apologia much like that in "The Author upon Himself" (1714) in the rest.

The imitation of Horace enables Swift to transform the complaints, defenses, and boastings which give "The Author upon Himself" such a querulous and ineffective tone into some of the most engaging passages anywhere in Swift's verse. In "The Author upon Himself" Swift glories in the fame and dignity his associations with the ministry have given him:

> At *Windsor S——* no sooner can appear,
> But, *St. John* comes and whispers in his Ear;
> The Waiters stand in Ranks; the Yeomen cry,
> *Make Room*; as if a Duke were passing by.
>
> (33-36)

The imitation proclaims Swift's importance just as emphatically: it shows "What I desire the World should know" (42)—that Swift was sent for by Harley, mingles "with Ribbons blew and green" (29), "rudely press[es] before a Duke" (39), and takes pleasure at being rebuked for it (40). Likewise, in "The Author upon Himself" Swift is "Admitted private, when Superiors wait" (30); in the imitation Swift "get[s] a Whisper, and withdraw[s]" (43). But the sense of self-importance is disguised in the imitation by the Horatian tone of reluctance and irritation, of desire for retreat. In "The Author upon Himself" Swift avows his influence—"In Favour grows with Ministers of State" (29)—and his goal: "The publick Int'rest to support" (27). Although in the imitation Swift follows Horace in deploring the "twenty Fools" who pursue him with petitions or requests (44), he is at least partially using Horace's sincere annoyance to disguise the same desire as in "The Author upon Himself," that his influence, power, and familiarity with the great be recognized:

> The Duke expects my Lord and you,
> About some great Affair, at Two—
> "Put my Lord *Bolingbroke* in Mind,
> "To get my Warrant quickly signed:
>
> .   .   .   .
>
> "I doubt not, if his Lordship knew—
> "And Mr. *Dean*, one Word from you—
>
> (53-62)

Much of "The Author upon Himself" defends Swift against those who attack his wit or influence. The imitation as a whole is a similar, but much more subtle defense: it protests, by example, that his wit is innocent—look how much he is like Horace, after all—and that he, like Horace, does not in fact have all the influence others ascribe to him. Throughout the imitation the message is the same as in the emotional and straightforward "Author upon Himself," but the effect is much different: cloaked with Horatian disdain and urbanity, the imitation pleads his case with much more finesse.

The heart of his defense is the marvelous passage describing his closeness to Harley. It shows Swift's verse style at its best, perfected by the influence of Horace's ease and familiarity. It captures natural thought and speech patterns and creates a varied movement by parenthetical statements and caesuras, long series of run-on lines and abrupt statements or questions, heavily multisyllabic lines or mostly monosyllabic ones, all restrained by the pattern of frequently recurring rhymes:

> 'Tis (let me see) three Years and more,
> (*October* next, it will be four)
> Since HARLEY bid me first attend,
> And chose me an humble Friend;
> Would take me in his Coach to chat,
> And question me of this and that;
> As, "What's a-Clock?" And, "How's the Wind?"
> "Whose Chariot's that we left behind?
> Or gravely try to read the Lines
> Writ underneath the Country *Signs*;
> Or, "Have you nothing new to day
> "From *Pope*, from *Parnel*, or from *Gay*?
> Such Tattle often entertains
> My Lord and me as far as *Stains*,
> As once a week we travel down
> To *Windsor*, and again to Town,
> Where all that passes, *inter nos*,
> Might be proclaim'd at *Charing-Cross*.
>   (63–80)

But this is, in fact, its own sort of glorying, though justified in part by the "requirements" of his Horatian model. The lines assert an intimacy with the great, an appreciation and accept- and for what he is rather than for what he can do for them. He is not just their hired scribbler: they *like* him, and this adds greatly to his sense of dignity and self-esteem; this too he desires "the World should know." Swift wants it both ways in the poem. He professes that he has no influence or inside knowledge, that he is just a friend, but he also asserts his value to the ministry: he must come up because he "will be *of Use*," "'Tis for the *Service of the Crown*" (13–15; italics added). The interesting thing is that the use of imitation allows him to have it both ways. The imitation of Horace makes the professed themes (retirement, friendship) seem the real ones and enables Swift to express his true feelings while concealing them behind conventional re-sponses.

Pope, in the "Advertisement" prefixed to the publication of the "complete" version of the poem in 1738, asserts that his imi-tations are markedly different from Swift's:

The World may be assured, this Publication is no way meant to inter-fere with the *Imitations* of *Horace* by Mr. *Pope*: His Manner, and that of Dr. *Swift* are so entirely different, that they can admit of no Invidious Comparison. The Design of the one being to sharpen the Satire, and open the Sense of the Poet; of the other to rend[er] his native *Ease* and *Familiarity* yet more easy and familiar.[26]

Pope is surely right that their manners of imitating are different. Pope follows his models closely, plays individual characters, lines, and words off against their counterparts for positive, satiric, or humorous effects, and shapes his themes through interaction with those of Horace. Swift adapts Horace's poems freely, show-ing little concern for a close or faithful rendering of the original. He takes advantage of the reader's awareness of Horace's themes and words, even following them closely where it is advanta-geous, but ignoring them where it is not. Swift's basic method is to use Horace to provide an undertone or counterpoint for his own poems, the development of which remains his primary concern. There is little in Swift of Pope's sense of identity with Horace, of the almost reverent treatment of the master. Pope alters his situations to fit Horace; Swift alters Horace to fit his situations. Pope sets up a reciprocal relationship with Horace:[27] he takes from Horace but gives back new insights, almost a fuller meaning, because of the close similarity and the verbal interaction between his poem and its model. Swift's relationship with Horace is totally receptive: he takes from Horace, uses him, turns him about with little reverence or respect, and gives back nothing in return. Yet Pope's assessment of Swift's "Design" is incorrect; that he did not fully understand Swift's intentions is indicated by his dissatisfaction with Swift's "incomplete" imitations of *Quinque dies* and *Hoc erat*. Swift was not, as Pope thought, just applying a paraphrased—easier and more familiar—version of Horace to a contemporary situation. Swift's applications of Horace were always strategic: not "opening" but "using" the "Sense of the Poet" to lighten, intensify, obscure, or bring out themes and ideas he could not handle as effectively in any other way.

II

The failure of critics to recognize the use of similar allusive techniques in "Cadenus and Vanessa" has led many to misunderstand or underrate the poem.[28] It has, inaccurately, been labeled private and temporary, "written for Vanessa, and not intended for publication."[29] It has been called casual and straightforward, history turned into tetrameter couplets and encased in a mythological frame. Biographers have spent more time on the poem than critics and have found, at the extreme, a "clear confession" of Swift's impotency, "dropped into the poem with Swiftian cunning" in the line "[Cadenus] understood not what was Love."[30] It has been accused of lacking depth and significance: "The treatment is fashionable and elegantly formal with a glossy film of urbanity."[31] Attention to the poem's allusions, however, will show that Swift achieves control, complexity, and comprehensiveness by drawing into the poem *The Art of Love* and the *Aeneid*. Early in the poem Venus sends her "dapper Clerk" to her library in search of a legal opinion:

> The Goddess soon began to see
> Things were not ripe for a Decree,
> And said she must consult her Books,
> The *Lovers Fleta's, Bractons, Cokes*.
> First to a dapper Clerk she beckon'd,
> To turn to *Ovid*, Book the Second;
> She then referr'd them to a Place
> In *Virgil* (*vide Dido*'s Case).
>
> (104–11)

These lines have usually been regarded as no more than humorous and have been passed by without further attention. But the continued importance, throughout the poem, of the works the dapper clerk pulled down suggests that Swift must have had Ovid and Virgil in mind as he developed the structure, characters, tone, and themes of "Cadenus and Vanessa."

The *Art of Love* was a rich influence on the poem. Structurally, it provided a source for the mythological framework (1–125, 828–89), with shepherds, nymphs, Venus, Cupid, darts, and fires of love. A court with men and women "Pleading before the *Cyprian* Queen" (2) is not found in Ovid, but in the early eighteenth century it could readily be associated with Ovid. The most popular contemporary translation of *The Art of Love*, by Dryden, Congreve, and Tate, was entitled *Ovid's Art of Love. In Three Books. Together with his Remedy of Love. Translated into English Verse By Several Eminent Hands. To which are added, The Court of Love, A Tale from Chaucer. And the History of Love.*[32] Swift's opening and closing scenes take fine advantage of the imaginative possibilities present here for combining Ovid's prescriptions for love, in *The Art of Love*, with the pseudo-Chaucer-

ian prosecution of lovers in *The Court of Love*. In tone, *The Art
of Love* supplements the poem's comic framework by setting up
much of its irony. The irony derives particularly from Ovid's
statement of purpose in Book I:

> You, who in *Cupid*'s Rolls inscribe your Name,
> First seek an Object worthy of your Flame;
> Then strive with Art, your Lady's Mind to gain:
> And last, provide your Love may long remain.
> On these three Precepts all my Work shall move:
> These are the Rules and Principles of Love.
>
> (I, 40–45)

The contrast between Ovid's attitude and intentions toward his
Corinna and Cadenus's feelings about Vanessa becomes the
most powerful and lasting irony in the poem. But the attitude of
all of Swift's men is so far from Ovid's man that a general irony
results, appearing most steadily in the wry, slightly comic manner in which the entire poem is narrated. Out of this ironic dis-
tance grows the final and most important influence of Ovid,
one that is basic to what Swift is saying thematically in the
poem. Apollo instructs Ovid as follows:

> First know your self; who to himself is known,
> Shall love with Conduct, and his Wishes crown.
>
> (II, 556–57)

Swift's theme, applicable to Cadenus and human nature in general, concerns the failure to attain Apollo's end. The poem
explores the consequences of a *lack* of self-awareness and self-acceptance, which so often stands in the way of a person's opening
himself or herself in love to another human being.

Venus introduces the second important line of allusions by referring her assistants to "a Place / In *Virgil*," namely, the fourth
book of the *Aeneid*. The second and fourth sections of Swift's
poem (126–303, 444–827) derive their structure, and to some
extent their tone, from Virgil's story of Aeneas and Dido. Swift
establishes the importance of the *Aeneid* by parallels in structure

and characters. First, he makes three passages in the second section of "Cadenus and Vanessa"—Venus presenting her scheme to Pallas (184–97), Pallas's agreement and bestowal of virtues on Vanessa (198–227), and Venus's joy in her prospects for Vanessa (228–49)—parallel the three passages in Virgil where Juno proposes her scheme for the marriage of Aeneas and Dido (IV, 90–104), where Venus agrees to it (IV, 105–13), and where Juno suggests uniting them in the cave during a storm (IV, 114–28). The similarities in structure, extending to both action and agents, are too striking to be coincidental. Second, he makes Vanessa closely analogous to "infelix Dido" (IV, 68 and elsewhere). Like Dido's, her life is affected by a dispute between two goddesses; like Dido, she falls in love because of the machinations of Cupid and Venus; and like Dido's, her love is directed toward a man unable to respond to it as completely as she wishes. Swift could expect, then, that his readers would respond to Vanessa as a Dido-figure, but a partially comic, possibly mock-heroic one.[33]

The view of Dido held by Swift's contemporaries was strongly influenced by the tradition of Ovid's *Heroides*, perpetuated and extended by courtly love conventions. The sympathetic admiration expressed in *The Court of Love* is typical:

> There *Dido*, that unhappy dying Queen,
> With false *Aeneas*, in one Piece was seen.[34]

Dryden complains about the influence of Ovid's interpretation of the Dido-Aeneas story: "*Ovid* takes it up after him, even in the same Age, and makes an ancient Heroine of *Virgil's* new-created *Dido*; Dictates a Letter for her just before her death, to the ingrateful Fugitive. . . . This passes indeed with his Soft Admirers, and gives him the preference to *Virgil* in their esteem."[35] But its pervasiveness is best shown by such passing references as Antony Blackwall's explanation of some lines by Dido which he quotes to illustrate the figure of speech "Doubt": "This Figure keeps the Soul in eager *Attention*, and moves all her Tenderness and Compassions for an unhappy Sufferer."[36] In keeping with the tradition that views Dido sympathetically, almost tragically, Swift presents Vanessa in section 2 as attractive and desirable. The qualities given her by the Graces (160–71) and the virtues bestowed upon her by Pallas (205–10) must be seen, at this point, as estimable. As Dido had to be attractive enough to win Aeneas, so Vanessa must be endowed with "ev'ry Virtue" (148), in order not only that men will fall down before her, but also that

> Womankind
> Wou'd by her Model form their Mind,
> And all their Conduct wou'd be try'd
> By her, as an unerring Guide.[37]
> (236–39)

Thus, the *Aeneid* and the body of interpretations that surround it, besides providing the structure for the love story in Swift's poem, also supply important suggestions about how characters and events in that story are to be viewed.

After Vanessa's confrontation with the "Croud of fashionable Fops" and the "Party . . . of glitt'ring Dames" in section 3 (304–443), the influence of the *Aeneid* returns in section 4. As the love story of Cadenus and Vanessa unfolds in this fourth and longest section (444–827), it runs parallel to the tragic love story in the *Aeneid*, which gives it depth and universality. The encounter of Cadenus and Vanessa in lines 568–817, in particular, is similar in structure to that of Aeneas and Dido in the *Aeneid*, IV, 279–499.

Once again Vanessa's similarity to Dido influences our response to her. Just as Dido became the unwitting victim of a conflict between two goddesses, so Vanessa suffers from the dispute between Venus and Pallas; Vanessa, like Dido, is the victim of "the Fates decree" (485); and, like Dido, she falls through the action of Cupid, specifically through his longing "To vindicate his Mother's Wrongs" (467). The poem, through the Dido analogy, treats Vanessa sympathetically; it also seeks to justify her in other ways. First, she stumbles into love while engaged in a laudable activity. As Dido was betrayed for her hospitality and charity to a stranger, so Vanessa,

> Searching in Books for Wisdom's Aid,
> Was, in the very Search, betray'd.
> (490–91)

Also, Cupid's act was not wholly capricious. As he took advantage of Dido's initial attraction to Aeneas, so he works upon an initial companionship and compatibility between Cadenus and Vanessa:

> I find, says he, she wants a Doctor,
> Both to adore her and instruct her;
> I'll give her what she most admires,
> Among those venerable Sires.
> (498–501)

Finally, and most importantly, her love does not result from "Want of Sense" (297). Like Dido, she was from birth a sensible, self-sufficient person. Pallas sowed

> within her tender Mind
> Seeds long unknown to Womankind,
> For manly Bosoms chiefly fit,
> The Seeds of Knowledge, Judgment, Wit.
> (202–5)

The fruits of those seeds are indicated by Cadenus's praise of her mind:

> *Ideas* came into her Mind
> So fast, his Lessons lagg'd behind:
> She reason'd, without plodding long,
> Nor ever gave her Judgment wrong.
> (556–59)

Cadenus uses that truth to rationalize his pride in her love for him:

> 'Tis Merit must with her prevail,
> He never knew her Judgment fail,
> She noted all she ever read,
> And had a most discerning Head.
> (754–57)

That she is the same person after falling in love as before is shown by the logic she uses in trying to win Cadenus's love.[38] Her "weighty Arguments to prove / That Reason was her Guide in Love" (676–77) exaggerate Cadenus's virtues but emphasize the fact that she regards his internal qualities as more important than his external ones. Vanessa's reasonableness is further emphasized by the ironic contrast between her and the Fops and Dames, who used the same terms in the preceding section:

> Their Judgment was upon the Whole,
> —That Lady is the dullest Soul—.
> (358–59)

> Discoursing with important Face,
> On Ribbons, Fans, and Gloves and Lace.
> (376–77)

> With all her Wit, I wou'd not ask
> Her Judgment, how to buy a Mask.
> (420–21)

The use of "Judgment" and "Discoursing" (i.e., discourse of reason) for determining trivial issues stresses Vanessa's superiority over the unthinking society around her. Her "Dignity" (595) and ability to distinguish "Right or Wrong" (599) confirm that she is worthy of Cadenus's love and well suited to him in every respect but age.

Dignified and reasonable though she may be, Vanessa is not and need not be wholly ideal and serious. Her excellence and beauty were emphasized in section 2 as a positive contrast to the Fops and Dames in section 3 and to Cadenus in section 4. Once that contrast is established, she can be satirized in section 4 without loss of the admirable qualities which make her fully worthy of Cadenus. She is a victim of love but, like Dido, not a faultless victim, and the poem rallies her failures—however temporary—to maintain inviolately the reasonableness that has set her apart from other women:

> Love can with Speech inspire a Mute,
> And taught *Vanessa* to dispute.
> This Topick, never touch'd before,
> Display'd her Eloquence the more:
> Her Knowledge, with such Pains acquir'd,
> By this new Passion grew inspir'd.
> Thro' this she made all Objects pass,
> Which gave a Tincture o'er the Mass.
> (712–19)

She is also twitted for expecting Cadenus to answer "every End, / The Book, the Author, and the Friend" (704–5), and for allowing her love to be tinged with hero worship (732–43) and self-love (681–87). But the narrator, always ironic but not always objective, exaggerates her excesses (and denigrates Cadenus at the same time) by the satiric comparisons he establishes:

> What Mariner is not afraid,
> To venture in a Ship decay'd?
> What Planter will attempt to yoke
> A Sapling with a falling Oak?
> (532–35; also 720–25)

Although Vanessa has faults, they are treated with a good deal of consideration and humor because they arise out of love and out of her desire to reach out to another person in a relationship which would not be wholly passionate or unreasonable.

Cadenus's character, too, is brought out by the allusions, particularly by his similarities to Aeneas. Like Aeneas, Cadenus, while pursuing his "mission" or "calling," meets a woman who becomes enamored of him; like Aeneas, he allows his relationship with that woman, whom he cannot love unreservedly, to proceed further than he actually intends; and like Aeneas, he has a mouthful of excuses as he breaks off that relationship. Dissimilarities, however, stand out just as sharply and contribute to the comic and self-satiric qualities of Swift's style. Unlike Aeneas, Cadenus is not princely and awe-inspiring but has "Declin'd in Health, advanc'd in Years" (529). Unlike Aeneas, he is not a hero surrounded by physical and moral dangers but "A Gownman of a diff'rent Make" (463) threatened only by some pupils, books, and state affairs. Unlike Aeneas, his refusal of the woman who loves him is not motivated by destiny and duty but comes because "his Dignity and Age / Forbid *Cadenus* to engage" (778–79). Cadenus's similarities to, and even his differences from, Aeneas reinforce the structural parallels between them and force upon Cadenus some of the stigma Aeneas has traditionally borne for his treatment of Dido.

The view of Aeneas held by Swift's contemporaries also was influenced by the wide acceptance of Ovid's reinterpretation of Virgil's tale. Dryden admits that Aeneas "is Arraign'd with more shew of Reason by the Ladies; who will make a numerous Party against him, for being false to Love, in forsaking *Dido*. And I cannot much blame them; for to say the truth, 'tis an ill Precedent for their Gallants to follow."[39] The blame, hinted at by Dryden and implicit in such epitaphs as "faith-less" Aeneas,[40] is made explicit by Joseph Trapp's notes to his translation of the *Aeneid*: "And therefore after all, *it was a Fault in him*, tho' he was *driven* to it by the Goddesses, *Juno*, and *Venus*. But . . . tho' their Impulse may in a great Measure *excuse* him, yet it does not *justify* him."[41] And it is accepted without question late in the century by so unromantic a writer as Samuel Johnson: "When Aeneas is sent by Virgil to the shades, he meets Dido the queen of Carthage, whom his perfidy had hurried to the grave."[42] By making Cadenus loosely and comically analogous to Aeneas, Swift gives Cadenus the principal responsibility for allowing his relationship with Vanessa to develop into an impossible situation.

In responding to the situation, Cadenus, like Aeneas, dis-

plays insensitivity and thoughtlessness. Cadenus is so wrapped
up in his world of "Politicks and Wit" (503) that other human
beings have become objects to be manipulated. He does not
recognize Vanessa as a complete and complex individual: he
had even "met her in a publick Place, / Without distinguishing
her Face" (634–35). He cares only for the pride and satisfaction
he derives from training her intellect:

> That innocent Delight he took
> To see the Virgin mind her Book,
> Was but the Master's secret Joy
> In School to hear the finest Boy.
> (550–53)

Cadenus has been playing roles so long, so self-protectively ("In
every *Scene* had kept his Heart" [541; italics added]), that he no
longer knows himself or others, and thus he fails to understand
his own actions and how another might respond to them. He
has deceived himself into thinking that his motivation is wholly
pedagogical. Actually, the situation is latently sexual, but he
keeps it on his terms, satisfying his desires without thought of
what the situation might mean or do to Vanessa. This self-de-
ception leads him unconsciously to encourage Vanessa's love—as
he probably has all along—by the pride he takes in her affection.

> His Pride began to interpose,
> Preferr'd before a Crowd of Beaux,
> So bright a Nymph to come unsought,
> Such Wonder by his Merit wrought.
> (750–53)

The "innocent Delight" he takes in trying to "form and cultivate
her Mind" (631), without concern for the rest of her person, illustrates the self-concern and pride that characterize Cadenus. It is
small wonder that as he begins to grasp the situation, he feels
"within him rise / Shame, Disappointment, Guilt, Surprize"
(624–25).

Once aware of Vanessa's love, aware of what is going on out-

side himself, he is unable to cope with it because of his lack of
self-understanding and self-acceptance. His first reaction is fear
of losing the self-image he has created and projected. Cadenus,
unlike Vanessa, is unable to live up to the theories about honesty
and self-assertion that he himself has professed:

> Two Maxims she could still produce,
> And sad Experience taught their Use:
> That Virtue, pleas'd by being shown,
> Knows nothing which it dare not own;
>
> .   .   .   .
>
> That common Forms were not design'd
> Directors to a noble Mind.[43]
> (606–13)

Vanessa is able to be herself, to accept what is, and to do the
right thing without fear of recriminations or consequences.
Cadenus, however, lacks the self-confidence to be able to face
the gossip society will engage in at his expense if their relationship progresses:

> Or grant her Passion be sincere,
> How shall his Innocence be clear?
> *Appearances* were all so strong,
> *The World* must think him in the Wrong;
> Wou'd say, He made a treach'rous Use
> Of Wit, to flatter and seduce:
> *The Town* wou'd swear he had betray'd,
> By Magick Spells, the harmless Maid;
> And *ev'ry Beau* wou'd have his Jokes,
> That Scholars were like other Folks.
>
> .   .   .   .
>
> Five thousand Guineas in her Purse?
> The Doctor might have fancy'd worse.
> (640–55; italics added)

It is a small man who cowers from such charges by such people.

His second reaction to Vanessa's declarations of love is to
offer friendship in return:

> But Friendship in its greatest Height,
> A constant, rational Delight,
> On Virtue's Basis fix'd to last,
> When Love's Allurements long are past;
> Which gently warms, but cannot burn;
> He gladly offers in return:
> His Want of Passion will redeem,
> With Gratitude, Respect, Esteem:
> With that Devotion we bestow,
> When Goddesses appear below.
> (780–89)

Swift may have valued friendship more highly than romantic love,[44] but he kept himself out of the poem sufficiently to avoid presenting his own ideal in an unqualified way. Cadenus's florid speech, filtered through the narrator's irony, indicates Swift's awareness that others may not be able to attain his ideal and may not even regard it as an ideal. In addition, the narrator hints, both in line 784, quoted above, and in the following passage, that Cadenus, in offering such friendship, is partially seeking to avoid the pitfalls of love:

> *Love*, why do we one Passion call?
> When 'tis a Compound of them all;
> . . . .
> Where Pleasures mix'd with Pains appear,
> Sorrow with Joy, and Hope with Fear.
> (772–77)

Friendship does not require the total surrender to and acceptance of another human being which love at its fullest does. If Cadenus is retreating from the risks of such openness, the position of friendship in the poem must be qualified. It is further qualified by the tone of Vanessa's reply, as she satirizes the excesses in Cadenus's offer:

> While thus *Cadenus* entertains
> *Vanessa* in exalted Strains,

> The Nymph in sober Words intreats
> A Truce with all sublime Conceits.
> For why such Raptures, Flights, and Fancies,
> To her, who durst not read Romances;
> In lofty Style to make Replies,
> Which he had taught her to despise.
> (790–97)

Friendship—constant, rational, safe—is fine for goddesses and perhaps for Swift, but it is admittedly "Seraphick" (823), and the narrator hints strongly that to "temper Love and Books together" (825) would be a satisfactory resolution for most mortals, Cadenus included.

The love story, in sum, treats Vanessa with a good deal of sympathy, as a Dido-figure who, though partially comic, loves deeply and understandably, and as one who seeks a love based on the lasting qualities of mental and spiritual compatibility, to which a difference in ages should not be an insurmountable barrier. Cadenus, on the other hand, is carefully and specifically linked to the other satiric targets in the poem. Like Venus in section 2, Cadenus is self-deceived (cf. 293 with 548–53), he acts out of pride (cf. 228 with 750 and 763), and he is a foolish projector (cf. 132, 289, 290, and 299 with 584–86). Like the Fops and Dames in section 3, he is egocentric and vain: as they show the shallowness and emptiness of society by their repudiation of Vanessa, Cadenus, by rejecting her, reveals his own foolishness and pride.

The finality of his rejection is clear in spite of lines 818–19:

> But what Success *Vanessa* met,
> Is to the World a Secret yet.

Although some critics have labeled the lines enigmatic or indecisive, the answer to them is implicit in lines 768–71 ("Love . . . Disdain'd to enter in so late") and 808–11:

> Tho' she already can discern,
> Her Scholar is not apt to learn;

Or wants Capacity to reach
The Science she designs to teach.

The futility of further attempts by Vanessa to gain Cadenus's love is evident.

Vanessa's failure leads, in the final section (828–89), to the reopening of the court case which Venus decrees "against the *Men*" (853) with the following explanation:

"She saw her Favour was misplac'd;
"The Fellows had a wretched Taste;
"She needs must tell them to their Face,
"They were a senseless, stupid Race.
(868–71)

The mythological framework reinforces and universalizes the themes particularized in the case of Cadenus and Vanessa. Because the fellows do not know themselves, they lose the trial and fail to attain Ovid's goal, to "love with Conduct, and [their] Wishes crown." Like Cadenus, the fellows lack self-understanding and self-acceptance; in their blindness they tried to shift onto others the guilt they could not face in themselves:

The Fault must on the *Nymphs* be plac'd,
Grown so corrupted in their Taste.
(65–66)

But the men are not blamed alone. Early in the poem Venus observed, in the poem's only triplet, that

there were but few
Of either Sex, among the Crew,
Whom she or her Assessors knew.
(101–3)

Self-centeredness and pride prevent both men and women from getting outside themselves and loving others. It is more than a jest; it is a serious moral indictment of human nature, as applicable to our day as to Swift's, when Venus must admit "That Mortals here disdain to love" (81).

The allusive matrix in "Cadenus and Vanessa" raises the poem from mere biography to a serious statement on love, self-understanding, and human nature. It is by no means "less remarkable . . . as a poem than as an autobiographical document,"[45] nor is it "impossible to believe that Swift would have done anything so unmeaning, so futile, as to write an account of the matter which was not strictly true."[46] To the extent that it was written for Esther Vanhomrigh, it was written rhetorically, with the facts shaped to fit Swift's strategy of complimenting Esther highly through his characterization of Vanessa, exaggerating her abilities and accomplishments, and admitting that she is not wrong in desiring or even expecting marriage, but indicating firmly all the while that marriage is out of the question for reasons that place most of the blame on himself. When it is seen to have more than just biographical implications, when it is seen to include an examination of the universal human need for self-acceptance and self-sacrifice in love—and the sad consequences of their absence—the poem becomes a remarkable work of art. It is difficult not to be impressed, even moved, by the reflection and introspection that led Swift to a deeper understanding of humankind as well as of his relationship with Esther.

Swift's rhetorical purposes in the Horatian imitations and "Cadenus and Vanessa" are achieved, to a large degree, through his handling of allusions. The allusive method in these poems enabled Swift to probe the depths of personal and emotional themes while maintaining a light and smooth surface; to create complexity below an apparent obviousness and clarity; and to generalize from an initially personal and/or temporary situation. In the earlier poems, allusions affected structure, tone, or theme, but separately. Now those effects are achieved simultaneously by making the allusions integral and active parts in the construction of the poems. Out of the union of allusion with tone and theme, together with the rapid, colloquial, tetrameter pace, comes a poetic blend which can be called distinctively Swiftian.

IV

The Arts of Love and Friendship
Swift's Poems about Women

In the Horatian imitations and "Cadenus and Vanessa" Swift began to use allusions to influence the form, tone, and total meaning of his poems. Such use of allusions became the basis of Swift's further development as a poet and a characteristic of his finest poems. The course of that development—not continuous, but very significant—is apparent in a series of poems about women written in or near the 1720s and characterized by similar techniques and interrelated themes. The earlier poems in this series are of interest for the way they present Swift's ideas about women clearly and directly, though they make only slight use of allusion and have little breadth or power. The later ones, poems of much more depth and significance and perhaps the best-known of Swift's poems, rely heavily on allusions for their impact. In this chapter we will consider Swift's poems about women individually and as a group, discussing first the "Progress" poems and the poems to Stella, then "To Lord Harley . . . on his Marriage," and then the "scatological" verse.

97

The Arts of Love and Friendship

I

The themes in Swift's poems about women are clarified by contrasting the "Progress" poems of 1719 and 1722 with the Stella poems, many of which were written about the same time and have similar themes and techniques. Both groups of poems use images of physical decay and mock-pastoral motifs to bring out the folly of overemphasizing the physical and emotional in human relationships. The "Progress" poems are satiric, exposing the delusiveness of the romantic and the physical; the Stella poems, as if in reply, stress the lasting, rational values of deeper relationships and establish Stella as the "Best Pattern of true Friends."[1]

Two passages in "A Letter to a Young Lady, on her Marriage" (1723) reflect nicely the contrasting approaches, images, and tones of "Phillis, Or, the Progress of Love" (1719), "The Progress of Beauty" (1719), and "The Progress of Marriage" (1722), on the one hand, and the poems to Stella on the other:

You have but a very few Years to be young and handsome in the Eyes of the World; and as few Months to be so in the Eyes of a Husband, who is not a Fool; for, I hope, you do not still dream of Charms and Raptures; which Marriage ever did, and ever will put a sudden End to. Besides, yours was a Match of Prudence, and common Good-liking, without any Mixture of that ridiculous Passion which hath no Being, but in Play-Books and Romances.

When you can bring yourself to comprehend and relish the good Sense of others, you will arrive, in Time, to think rightly yourself, and to become a reasonable and agreeable Companion. This must produce in your Husband a true rational Love and Esteem for you, which old Age will not diminish. He will have a Regard for your Judgment and Opinion, in Matters of the greatest Weight; you will be able to entertain each other, without a third Person to relieve you, by finding Discourse.[2]

More striking than Swift's vendetta against romance is his vision of such a friendship as he describes occurring between the sexes. It is one thing for Swift to say of Addison that "often as they spent their evenings together, they neither of them ever wished for a third person, to support or enliven their conversation."[3] It is quite another thing to expect the same of a man and woman, a husband and wife.

In their development of these themes the "Progress" poems and the poems to Stella do not rely to any significant extent on allusions. There are indeed passing verbal allusions, as to Diana in "The Progress of Beauty," and allusions to various classical figures, as in the birthday poem to Stella, 1724/25:

> No Poet ever sweetly sung,
> Unless he were like *Phœbus*, young;
> Nor ever Nymph inspir'd to Rhyme,
> Unless, like *Venus*, in her Prime.
> At Fifty six, if this be true,
> Am I a Poet fit for you?
> Or at the Age of Forty three,
> Are you a Subject fit for me?
> (19–26)

There is also, in the Stella poems, a sketchy pattern of allusions to classical philosophy, established by passing references to scholars, "tedious Moralists," Stoics, sages, Cato, and Socrates, and supported by an emphasis on truth ("true" and "truth" are used at least twenty times in the poems). Several such words combine in some key lines from "To Stella, Who Collected and Transcribed his Poems" (1720):

> Now should my Praises owe their Truth
> To Beauty, Dress, or Paint, or Youth,
> What Stoicks call *without our Power*,
> They could not be insur'd an Hour.
>
> .   .   .   .
>
> Your Virtues safely I commend,
> They on no Accidents depend:
> Let Malice look with all her Eyes,
> She dares not say the Poet lyes.
> (61–64, 79–82)

The attack on fleeting external beauties, with the implied authority of classical philosophy, versus the commendation of lasting
internal worth, and the juxtaposition of "lyes" with the "Truth,"
sum up nicely the contrasts between the ladies of the "Progress"
poems and the lady of the Stella poems. Such allusions, brief
and casual though they are, reinforce the reasonable, reflective
tone which is crucial to the form and theme of the poems to
Stella.

Swift supplements those passing references by weaving into
the poems parallels to or echoes of the kind of ancient wisdom
popularized by the translations and paraphrases of L'Estrange.[4]
In the final birthday poem (1727/28), for example, the central
theme, "by all Sages" and by "stubborn Stoicks" understood
(27, 50), is that a virtuous life will be a support in old age:

> [Virtue should] leave behind
> Some lasting Pleasure in the Mind,
> Which by Remembrance will assuage,
> Grief, Sickness, Poverty, and Age.
> (29–32)

As Swift goes on to ask, "Say, *Stella*, feel you no Content, / Reflecting on a Life well spent?" (35–36), the lines parallel a passage
in Cicero's *Cato Major*: "The only Weapons to fence with against
Age are moral Accomplishments and virtuous Habits. If these
are secur'd and cultivated betimes, 'tis not to be imagin'd, what
Encouragement and Sufficiency they'll afford at the latter End
of the Day. . . . Besides, the Answer of a good Conscience, upon
the Review of a Man's Life and Conversation, is the noblest
Refreshment in the World."[5] The echoing of a classical philoso-
pher strengthens the argument of the poem by proof from authority and contributes significantly to its logical, thoughtful mood.

That these parallels, which cannot properly be called allusions, are integral to the poems is shown by the way Swift uses
such a reference to establish the fundamental theme of the Stella
poems. Swift includes the following lines in the first birthday
poem (1718/19):

> So little is thy Form declin'd
> Made up so largly in thy Mind.
>   (7–8)

This clearly is not *form* in the Aristotelian sense of Johnson's first definition, "the external appearance of any thing," under which he quotes lines from "The Progress of Beauty." Rather, it is the Platonic sense of definition 12, the "true essential form," illustrated by a quotation from Bacon: "They inferred, if the world were a living creature, it had a soul and spirit, by which they did not intend God, for they did admit of a deity besides, but only the soul or essential *form* of the universe." Form, then, is the intrinsic principle which determines a thing; and Swift uses this bit of Platonism to declare that the Stella that matters is internal. Thus, Stella's body may grow older, her locks turn grey and wrinkles appear, but "No Length of Time can make you quit" the "Honour and Virtue, Sense and Wit" that constitute the essential Stella.[6] The contrast to Diana or Celia in "The Progress of Beauty," whose forms can be discussed only in the Aristotelian sense, is striking:

> And Form, say I, as well as They,
> Must fayl if Matter brings no Grist.
>
> And this is fair Diana's Case.
>   (83–85)

In these lines the interlocking but contrasting themes of the poems about women during the 1720s come out most clearly. The satire in the "Progress" poems on the romantic and "accidental" falsities of external appearances is answered in the Stella poems by the truth—expounded by the ancients and valid for all times—that inner qualities of mind and soul, because they are enduring, should be of prime concern to both men and women.

Allusions in these poems, on the whole, are less carefully developed and less influential than those in the Horatian imitations and "Cadenus and Vanessa." The "Progress" poems and the poems to Stella were written after Swift's exile to Ireland. They came at a time when Swift was giving his main attention to social concerns and to several major projects in prose, including *Gulliver's Travels*, and he ceased for a time to give poetry the serious attention necessary for continued development of the skills he had been learning in 1712 and 1713. He produced many casual and enjoyable poems, but few major ones, in the decade between 1715 and 1725. Because they were written during this hiatus in Swift's development as a serious poet, the poems discussed above are valuable in illustrating, by contrast, the importance of allusion in Swift's poetry. This can be shown most readily by going back to an earlier poem, then on to a later group of poems about women. Witty and vivid though they are, the "Progress" poems and the poems to Stella lack the depth and sophistication, in thought and theme, of the marriage poem to Harley and the scatological poems.

II

Although it is addressed "To Lord Harley . . . on his Marriage," Swift's epistle to Robert Harley's son is equally a poem about women. Written about the same time (1713) as the Horatian imitations and "Cadenus and Vanessa," it reflects the techniques developed in the former and the themes explored in the latter.

The poem is unified by its allusions to Ovid. To organize the opening theme of praise to Harley, Swift uses the tale of Daphne and Apollo from the first book of the *Metamorphoses*.

> The God of Wit, and Light, and Arts,
> With all acquir'd and nat'ral parts,
> Whose harp could savage beasts enchant,
> Was an unfortunate gallant.

.   .   .   .

> Ten thousand footsteps, full in view,
> Mark out the way where Daphne flew.
> (9–12, 17–18)

Swift adapts the story to his purposes by supplying a motivation not present in Ovid. Daphne rejects and flees from Apollo *because of* his intelligence and parts: "Yet Daphne never slack'd her pace, / For wit and learning spoil'd his face" (27–28). This affords Swift a springboard for both compliment and satire. It elevates Edward Harley by analogy, as it endows him with the qualities of Apollo; and it establishes a basis for satire against society, against men who lack the qualities of Harley and against women who fail to appreciate them:

> For such is all the sex's flight,
> They fly from learning, wit, and light:
> They fly, and none can overtake
> But some gay coxcomb, or a rake.
> (19–22)

Harley's success in winning the hand of Lady Henrietta Cavendish Holles contrasts with the unsuccessful amours of Apollo and with the context in which the story of Daphne and Apollo appears in the first book of Ovid. The succession of passionate, brutal, illicit sexual encounters there adds to the significance, from moral and social perspectives, of the lawful, decorous, suitable marriage Swift is celebrating.

The allusions to Ovid, as a basis for contrasts of individual and society, continue in the latter half of the poem, which is given to praise of the lady. Because "Ca'ndish," unlike Daphne, accepts her proper role and place, Swift can juxtapose the two. Daphne, tempted with "The chief among that glitt'ring crowd, / Of titles, birth, and fortune proud" (39–40), might have yielded, as she probably would have done had Bacchus or Mars pursued her instead of Apollo (13–16). But Lady Cavendish, supported by the endowments of Pallas which Swift prized in women, stands firm against such temptations:

> The Nymph, with indignation, view'd
> The dull, the noisy, and the lewd:
> For Pallas, with celestial light,
> Had purify'd her mortal sight.
>
> (47–50)

She responds instead to the "Virtues all combin'd" (51) in Harley's mind. Her choice and the basis on which she made it turn to compliments on the character and virtue of Harley and on her own good sense as well. That good sense is complimented once more by reference to the story of Daphne and Apollo:

> Terrestrial nymphs, by formal arts,
> Display their various nets for hearts:
> Their looks are all by method set,
> When to be prude, and when coquette;
>
> .   .   .   .
>
> But, when a Goddess would bestow
> Her love on some bright youth below,
> Round all the earth she casts her eyes.
>
> (53–56, 59–61)

The negative connotations of "arts" and "nymphs" are opposed to the open search of the goddesses, and the contrast is brought to bear on the idea of choice. Wrapped up in thoughts of arts and skills, Daphne-like mortals cannot respond with the will: "Yet, wanting skill and pow'r to chuse, / Their only pride is to refuse" (57–58). Lady Cavendish, goddesslike in values and understanding, by contrast, "Makes choice of him she fancies best, / And bids the ravish'd youth be bless'd" (63–64). Through its allusions, then, the greater part of the poem is given to praise of the couple, not just for the usual traits of beauty, grace, and wealth, but for understanding, good sense, and virtue.

Allusions are also Swift's chief means for relating the piece to the marriage-poem tradition. Early in the poem the tale of Daphne and Apollo introduces the marriage theme; later the antithetical myths of Aurora and Tithonus and of Selene and Endymion draw in through symbol the traditional concerns of marriage poems. Although Swift's poem, because it focuses on the appropriateness of a marriage rather than celebrates a wedding, is not properly an epithalamium, it does include several characteristics of that form. Use of the goddesses of dawn and of the moon focuses on the usual motif of day and night, though not specifically the traditional wedding day and night. But the sexual theme usually brought out by the latter is present anyway, drawn in by allusions. The contrasting characters of the two goddesses—to both of whom Lady Cavendish is compared—give her a sense of chaste sensuality. Aurora is notorious for her amorousness: "For Aphrodite caused Dawn to be perpetually in love, because she had bedded with Ares."[7] Diana, on the other hand, who in time came to replace Selene as the goddess in the Endymion myth, has always symbolized chastity. Through his allusions Swift was able to introduce the sexual side of marriage discreetly and to approve Lady Cavendish's virtue without depriving her of vitality: "Ca'ndish, as Aurora bright, / And chaster than the Queen of Night" (77–78). Finally, the allusions remind one of the traditional marriage-poem wishes for long life and happiness. In both the Aurora and Diana myths the longevity of the spouse is a key feature; by Swift's pairing of them, the unfortunate effects of Aurora's failure to request perpetual youth as well as immortality for her husband are balanced by the enduring youth and beauty bestowed on Endymion by Selene's love. All of these traditional motifs, the allusions suggest, are part of the blessings that descend on "A Mortal of superior kind" (80) when he is accepted by a nymph of superior sense and character.

Thus, the allusions in "To Lord Harley . . . on his Marriage" give shape to its structure and depth to its theme and tone. Allusions direct the poem, with grace and a bit of subtlety, toward approval of the same traits of character and behavior which Swift endorsed directly and even didactically, without the help of allusive structures, in the "Progress" poems and the poems to Stella.

III

More than a decade after the "Progress" poems and several years after the last of the Stella poems, Swift wrote yet another series of poems about women. He never refers to them in his letters or says elsewhere why he wrote them or what he intended by them. A clue is provided, however, by an allusion on the title page of *A Beautiful Young Nymph Going to Bed. Written for the Honour of the Fair Sex. . . . To which are added, Strephon and Chloe. And Cassinus and Peter*, a quarto pamphlet published by Roberts in 1734. Below the first title Swift added, "Pars minima est ipsa Puella sui. Ovid *Remed. Amoris*."[8] The epigraph suggests that Swift set out to write his own remedies for love, for the erotic, romantic love attacked in the "Progress" poems and disparaged in the poems to Stella. His "remedies" were to be, like Ovid's, comic poems with an underlying seriousness. But Swift, unlike Ovid, could not maintain a light, dispassionate attitude toward his subject matter. As a result, tone in the scatological poems is not defined as sharply as in the earlier poems on women, but theme is conveyed with more depth and power because of allusions.

The line quoted in the epigraph—"A woman is the least part of herself"—is aimed specifically at "A Beautiful Young Nymph," but its context applies more directly to the earliest of the group, "The Lady's Dressing Room" (1730). Here, Strephon is turned into a total misogynist by his close survey of the contents of and implements in Celia's dressing chamber and by his discovery, in particular, of the unemptied "Chest." Ovid gives, as his ultimate remedy for passion, the following prescription: "When she is painting her cheeks with concoctions of dyes, go (let not shame hinder you) and see your mistress' face. Boxes you will find, and a thousand colours, and juices that melt and drip into her warm bosom. Such drugs smell of your table, Phineus; not once only has my stomach grown queasy at them."[9] The passage has obvious affinities to that in which Strephon surveys the litter after

Celia, "Array'd in Lace, Brocades and Tissues" (4), issues forth
for what is left of the day:

> Here Gallypots and Vials plac'd,
> Some fill'd with Washes, some with Paste,
> Some with Pomatum, Paints and Slops,
> And Ointments good for scabby Chops.
> Hard by a filthy Bason stands,
> Fowl'd with the Scouring of her Hands;
> The Bason takes whatever comes
> The Scrapings of her Teeth and Gums.
>
> . . . .
>
> But oh! it turn'd poor *Strephon*'s Bowels,
> When he beheld and smelt the Towels.
>   (33–44)

Ovid's prescription, intended to temper a passion for a specific
woman, was not designed to have the general effect this experience
has on Strephon, whose "foul Imagination" henceforth "links /
Each Dame he sees with all her Stinks: / And, if unsav'ry Odours
fly, / Conceives a Lady standing by" (121–24).

Swift surely meant the scene this poem presents as comic,
with its discrepancies between Celia's orderly appearance when
she leaves the room and the confusion she leaves behind, and
between Strephon's naïve adoration of the sex before his inventory and his disillusioned misogyny after. Other parts of the
poem contribute to the comedy, particularly the analogies and
allusions used in describing "the Chest" (70).

> As from within *Pandora*'s Box,
> When *Epimetheus* op'd the Locks,
> A sudden universal Crew
> Of humane Evils upwards flew;
> He still was comforted to find
> That *Hope* at last remain'd behind;
> So *Strephon* lifting up the Lid,
> To view what in the Chest was hid.
> The Vapours flew from out the Vent,

> But *Strephon* cautious never meant
> The Bottom of the Pan to grope,
> And fowl his Hands in Search of *Hope*.
> O never may such vile Machine
> Be once in *Celia*'s Chamber seen!
> O may she better learn to keep
> "Those Secrets of the hoary deep!
> (83–98)

Here is Swift the storyteller at his best, pacing the account skill-fully, building up carefully to the punch lines in 94 and 98, and using allusions to increase the wit and satire. Not only do the allusions put excretion in proper perspective—by contrast to the enormous evils released by Epimetheus or Pandora and by Sin—but they also extend the limits of the "remedy." The Pandora legend, from its earliest available account in Hesiod, stands as a warning against woman as a snare, a punishment, the source of the evils in the world:

Forthwith the famous Lame God moulded clay in the likeness of a modest maid, as the son of Cronos purposed. . . . And Pallas Athene bedecked her form with all manner of finery. Also the Guide, the Slayer of Argus, contrived within her lies and crafty words and a de-ceitful nature. . . . And [Zeus] called this woman Pandora [the All-endowed], because all they who dwelt on Olympus gave each a gift, a plague to men who eat bread.[10]

And the allusion to *Paradise Lost* brings in the duplicity of women, as Satan's daughter, Sin, unlocks the Adamantine Gates, open-ing to view "The secrets of the hoarie deep" (II, 891), and releases sin and death from their confinement. In each case the outra-geousness of Swift's application renders the potentially serious allusion comic. And in each case the allusion provides a witty anticipation of Strephon's fate, for in the end he has no hope for good in women and is able to see only chaos and anarchy (*PL*, II, 895–96) in them, refusing to see or credit the "order" behind.

But the poem as a whole is not successful comedy, mostly because Swift was unable to disassociate himself sufficiently from
his material. Swift, of course, is not Strephon; critics over the
past few decades have argued this convincingly. But attempts to
show that Swift is emotionally detached from the subject matter
have been less convincing.[11] The intensity in tone of the lists
and details of the first half of the poem belie such claims. The
sounds, as well as the sights, convey a harshness that is not at
all dispassionate. *Listen*, for example, to these lines: "Allum
Flower to stop the Steams, / Exhal'd from sour unsavoury
Streams" (27–28); "For here she spits, and here she spues" (42);
"Begumm'd, bematter'd, and beslim'd" (45). The effect of Swift's
choice and arrangement of words and sounds is too harsh for
humor. There is a similar uncertainty in the cooking analogy:

> As Mutton Cutlets, Prime of Meat,
> Which tho' with Art you salt and beat,
> As Laws of Cookery require,
> And toast them at the clearest Fire;
> If from adown the hopeful Chops
> The Fat upon a Cinder drops . . . .
>   (99–104)

The opening lines are comic, with their ironic comparison of
the smells of food and excrement, an association reinforced (perhaps unintentionally) by the phrase "the *hope*ful Chops." Allusions extend the playfulness. Faulkner's edition glosses line 99
with *"Prima Virorum"*—a playful twist, I believe, on Dryden's
phrase characterizing Aeneas, "O best of Men"[12]—and glosses
"adown" in line 103 with a derisive glance at the style of Daniel
and Phillips: "Vide D[ea]n D[aniel']s Works, and N[amby]
P[amb]y's." As the passage continues, however, the words and
sounds become too intense to remain comic:

> To stinking Smoak it turns the Flame
> Pois'ning the Flesh from whence it came;

> And up exhales a greasy Stench,
> For which you curse the careless Wench.
>
> (105–8)

The scene strongly suggests sensations personally offensive to the poet, and the suggestion carries over to the tone of the inventory. Something besides comedy is going on here; deeper feelings of the author are showing through and are working against the comic effects.

Swift's epigraph on the title page links "A Beautiful Young Nymph Going to Bed" with this passage in Ovid's *Remedia Amoris*: "It will profit, too, of a sudden, when she has not prepared herself for anyone, to speed of a morning to your mistress. We are won by dress; all is concealed by gems and gold; a woman is the least part of herself. . . . Arrive unexpectedly: safe yourself, you will catch her unarmed: she will fall, hapless woman, by her own defects" (341–48 [p. 201]). Swift's poem, generally dated 1731, which follows a prostitute to her rooms and describes in detail her false appearance and real afflictions, is a remedy for lust rather than for love. Ovid disrobes a mistress for the purpose of controlling or limiting, not ending, the passion for her; Swift strips a whore for the apparent purpose of squelching all desire for any such women:

> Then, seated on a three-legg'd Chair,
> Takes off her artificial Hair:
> Now, picking out a Crystal Eye,
> She wipes it clean, and lays it by.
> Her Eye-Brows from a Mouse's Hyde,
> Stuck on with Art on either Side.
>
> .   .   .   .
>
> Now dextrously her Plumpers draws,
> That serve to fill her hollow Jaws.
> Untwists a Wire; and from her Gums
> A Set of Teeth completely comes.
> Pulls out the Rags contriv'd to prop
> Her flabby Dugs and down they drop.

. . . .
> Up goes her Hand, and off she slips
> The Bolsters that supply her Hips.
>
> (9-28)

Swift's intent, again, would seem to be comic: the discrepancy between the seeming Corinna and the actual one is exposed; Corinna certainly is the least part of herself.

What is in reality a sad situation, in the passage quoted above, is made amusing by the wit and lightness with which it is presented. In contrast to "The Lady's Dressing Room," the sounds in the lines often work to keep the reader from taking the scene seriously: "Never did *Covent Garden* boast / So bright a batter'd, strolling Toast" (3-4); "Pulls out the Rags contriv'd to prop / Her flabby Dugs and down they drop" (21-22); "And *Puss* had on her Plumpers p——st" (62). A pseudopastoral motif enhances the generally comic discrepancies: Corinna is neither "Nymph" (title, 65) nor "Goddess" (23); her fourth-floor lodging is no "Bow'r" (8); and, as the poem itself emphasizes, for her "no Shepherd sighs in vain" (2). When Corinna removes her "Crystal Eye" (11, 61), the poem gives comic concreteness to a metaphor that had praised many a damsel before her:

> Her eye seen in the tears, tears in her eye,
> Both crystals.
>
> Go, clear thy crystals.[13]

The mock pastoralism introduces a theme of art versus nature which is basic to the passage from Ovid and to all the scatological poems: "But how shall I describe her Arts / To recollect the scatter'd Parts?" (67-68).

Despite the successful comic elements and the apparent comic intent of the whole, much of the poem is not comic at all. A good many lines invite sympathy for Corinna.

> With gentlest Touch, she next explores
> Her Shankers, Issues, running Sores.
>
> (29-30)

The list of ailments may be intended to cause the reader to be amused or repulsed, but the reference to "gentlest Touch" wrenches the poem from its light, detached treatment and makes the reader realize that the object with artificial hair, false teeth, and flabby breasts is a human being. Likewise, in spite of the paradox in the phrase "With Pains of Love," the words following—"tormented lies" (39)—as well as the dream, in which she "feels the Lash, and faintly screams" (42), produce a sympathetic response in any sensitive reader and do not fit with the comic elements.

Swift's difficulties in controlling his tone and achieving a unified effect in the poem are best illustrated by the allusion to the *Aeneid* in line 46:

> Or, by a faithless Bully drawn,
> At some Hedge-Tavern lies in Pawn;
> Or to *Jamaica* seems transported,
> Alone, and by no Planter courted.
>
> (43–46)

From the first edition, a line on Dido was included as a footnote: "Longam incomitata videtur / ire viam" ["she seems to be . . . ever wending, companionless, an endless way"].[14] Several clear parallels to *Aeneid* IV are apparent, always with a reductive twist. Dido dreams of wandering alone in a desert seeking her subjects; Corinna has an evil vision of being in Jamaica "Alone, and by no Planter courted." Dido's dream is the result of a tragedy of love; Corinna's nightmare is caused by the "Pains of Love." Dido sees a series of dire portents concerning the future; Corinna has premonitions of Bridewell or other imprisonment. Dido goes to the "honour'd Chapel" to pray; Corinna goes to Fleet-Ditch, "on watch to lye" (49). The situation is latent with mock-heroic possibilities, as the nightmares of a quean are compared to the visions of a queen. The discrepancy of high versus low, dignified versus debased, is certainly present, but Swift did not take into account the effect of having the readers' sympathetic response to Dido carry over to Corinna: in her dream, after all, she, like Dido, is a victim of a man's infidelity. Described objectively, her jilting by a "faithless Bully" could have seemed ironically appropriate; but presented as it is, from Corinna's viewpoint, it produces sympathy. It, and the entire analogy of Corinna to Dido, is amusing intellectually, but the comedy is undercut by the emotional response. Swift's remedy for lust apparently called for readers to be amused at or repulsed by Corinna: "*Corinna* in the Morning dizen'd, / Who sees, will spew; who smells, be poison'd" (73–74). For either response, sympathy is fatal, yet sympathy there is. Readers have been so perplexed by the poem, and responded so differently to it, because Swift was unable to unify the work and elicit a single effect by it.[15]

"Strephon and Chloe," also dated 1731, is an account of and comment on the disillusionment of an ordinary mortal who marries an ethereal goddess, only to find, on his wedding night, that she is as human as himself. The Strephon of this poem might have been saved the consequences of his sudden enlightenment if he had had an experience similar to that of the Strephon of an earlier poem:

> O *Strephon*, e'er that fatal Day
> When *Chloe* stole your Heart away,
> Had you but through a Cranny spy'd
> On House of Ease your future Bride,
> In all the Postures of her Face,
> Which Nature gives in such a Case;
> Distortions, Groanings, Strainings, Heavings;
> Twere better you had lickt her Leavings,
> Than from Experience find too late
> Your Goddess grown a filthy Mate.
> Your Fancy then had always dwelt
> On what you saw, and what you smelt;
> Would still the same Ideas give ye,
> As when you spy'd her on the Privy.
> ("Strephon and Chloe," 235–48)

John M. Aden is right when he says these lines would "come closer to fitting a poem like 'The Lady's Dressing Room,' where the lesson would be more dramatically consistent."[16] They are included, however, to make "Strephon and Chloe" thematically consistent with the other scatological poems as remedies for love.

The comic intent of the poem is unmistakable, and the first 218 lines are good comedy. The story has a fine pace, an even tone, excellent balancing of detail, and an appropriate reversal. There is rollicking farce as well as verbal wit, all built up in a series of ironic juxtapositions. Descriptions of Chloe's goddess-like perfections are set over against deliberate references to the unpleasant characteristics she avoids. Thus, lines 9–10 are paired with 11–12:

> And then, so nice, and so genteel;
> Such Cleanliness from Head to Heel:
> No Humours gross, or frowzy Steams,
> No noisom Whiffs, or sweaty Streams.

And lines 15, 17, and 19 are contrasted with 16, 18, and 20:

> Would so discreetly Things dispose,
> None ever saw her pluck a Rose.
> Her dearest Comrades never caught her
> Squat on her Hams, to make Maid's Water.
> You'd swear, that so divine a Creature
> Felt no Necessities of Nature.

References to "Arm-pits," "Dog-Days," and smelly toes form the background against which her irreproachable cleanliness stands out (22–24).

Such verbal juxtaposings are mirrored by larger, structural ones, of passage against passage, to show how far from reality Strephon and Chloe are. The description of the wedding introduces contrasts of the literary with the real, the figurative with the literal, the knowing with the naïve.

> Imprimis, at the Temple Porch
> Stood *Hymen* with a flaming Torch.
>
> .   .   .   .
>
> The Muses next in Order follow,
> Conducted by their Squire, *Apollo:*
> Then *Mercury* with Silver Tongue,
> And *Hebe*, Goddess ever young.
> Behold the Bridegroom and his Bride,
> Walk Hand in Hand, and Side by Side;
> She by the tender Graces drest,
> But, he by *Mars*, in Scarlet Vest.
> (47–60)

The couple's awareness of themselves, of each other, and of their new state is as shallow as the allusions to the classical gods and goddesses, listed so properly and conventionally. Enclosing this highly romantic portrait of the marriage are two contrasting passages. The marriage was arranged in a most unromantic fashion; literalization of trite metaphors and verbal irony emphasize the materialism involved:

> But, *Strephon* sigh'd so loud and strong,
> He blew a Settlement along:
> And, bravely drove his Rivals down
> With Coach and Six, and House in Town.
> The bashful Nymph no more withstands,
> Because her dear Papa commands.
> (39–44)

The conclusion of the wedding is also marked by the material ("the Parson paid" [67]) and the physical ("now the Pair must *crown their Joys*" [70]). The words Swift italicized epitomize the dichotomy, as the trite euphemism covers over the physical reality. And the speaker's concrete language, as he describes the dilemma facing Strephon after the wedding, contrasts with Strephon's literary abstractness:

> But, what if he should lose his Life
> By vent'ring *on* his heav'nly Wife.
>   (103–4)

The naïve Strephon is almost surely unaware, and the knowing speaker almost as surely fully aware, of the old double entendre the lines contain.

The juxtapositions of ideal and real extend into the romantic, conventional explanation of Chloe's hesitation in lines 145–60 (e.g., "Resistance on the Wedding-Night / Is what our Maidens claim by Right"), underscored by the allusion to the prayer book with its suggestion of perfect virtue: "And, *Chloe*, 'tis by all agreed, / Was Maid in Thought, and Word, and Deed." In contrast stands the real explanation, in lines 161–92: "The Bride must either void or burst." The contrast is sustained in the disparity between conventional marriage portraits, with cupids and a pastoral setting (193–202), and the disillusionment that sets in (203–18) as Strephon hears "the fuming Rill" (175). It is not a one-way disillusionment—if Strephon has lost his nymph, Chloe has lost her swain, and both experience a violent reaction against their previous idealism:

> Now *Strephon* daily entertains
> His *Chloe* in the homeli'st Strains;
> And, *Chloe* more experienc'd grown,
> With Int'rest pays him back his own.
>   (211–14)

Mock-heroic allusions to *Paradise Lost* throughout this section indicate the unimportance of the whole affair and the folly of the couple. The tone is raised to a pseudo-Miltonic level by similes and learned allusions. The woman "falls" first and the man, "Inspir'd with Courage from his Bride" (189), follows her example. The cupids fly away like the guardian angels, and chaotic bickering and strife set in. The comic analogue serves as an implicit comment on the episode: the poem, to this point, is not a manifestation of Swift's "profound dissatisfaction with woman,"[17] but a witty synopsis of the petty follies of human-kind.

Had the poem ended there, "Strephon and Chloe" would have been a successful, lightly satiric comic poem. But the poem continues for an additional ninety-six lines, very different from the earlier ones in style and effect. The final section is unrelieved didacticism, making explicit the lesson which was clearly implicit in the first section. The message—stated very effectively, at times—is the same as in the other poems about women:

> On Sense and Wit your Passion found,
> By Decency cemented round;
> Let Prudence with Good Nature strive,
> To keep Esteem and Love alive.
> Then come old Age whene'er it will,
> Your Friendship shall continue still:
> And thus a mutual gentle Fire,
> Shall never but with Life expire.
>
> (307–14)

But that lesson was clear already in the dramatic part of the poem: it did not need spelling out in a coda half as long as the story. And the concluding section contains no allusions, in striking contrast to the first part of the poem, which relied heavily on allusions to develop the structure and wit that make it so appealing. The final ninety-six lines of heavy-handed sermonizing, in sum, destroy the unity of the poem and, by not letting the situation speak for itself, reduce greatly the effectiveness of the work as a whole.

The final section of "Strephon and Chloe" also exposes an inconsistency in Swift's purposes in the scatological poems: the need, implied in the poems, to know but not to get too near the realities in question. In line 253 Swift calls defecation a "Blemish" which, decency requires, must be hidden; he reiterates this in lines 307–14, where "Decency" is called the cement that holds a friendship together. Men must, apparently, be aware that women do have such a "natural Defect" (274), but women must take great care that men are never confronted by it:

> Since Husbands get behind the Scene,
> The Wife should study to be clean;
> Nor give the smallest Room to guess
> The Time when Wants of Nature press.
>   (137–40)

There is no evidence that these lines are ironic. They appear to
bring out personal feelings of the author and reveal, despite the
frequent use of scatology in his verse and prose, a certain uneasiness with the subject. Ovid, further along in *Remedia Amoris*,
writes: "He who says o'er much 'I love not' is in love" (648 [p.
221]). Perhaps it is the same with one who says o'er much that
excretion does not bother him. Such an uneasiness leads to the
emphasis on discreetness in the poems, a greater emphasis,
probably, than is called for. The offensive or potentially offensive should not be ignored but should be hidden, kept behind
the scenes:

> To him that looks behind the Scene,
> *Satira*'s but some pocky Quean.
>   ("The Lady's Dressing Room," 133–34)[18]

"*Satira*" in the Williams edition is a misprint for "*Statira*," which
"contrasts Lee's virtuous queen [in *The Rival Queens*] with the
'pocky' actress who plays the role."[19] Surely one must not be so
naïve as to confuse the character with the actress. But Swift
seems to be asking whether one will appreciate the play any better for having seen the cast before they are made up. Elsewhere
he suggests that one will not:

> Why is a handsome Wife ador'd
> By ev'ry Coxcomb, but her Lord?
> From yonder Puppet-Man inquire,
> Who wisely hides his Wood and Wire.
>   ("Strephon and Chloe," 283–86)

Women should, then, keep men "deluded," not "By help of Pencil, Paint and Brush," but through the "utmost Cleanlyness"
and the greatest decency.[20]

The scatological poems are the natural successors to the "Progress" poems, both of which satirize the overemphasis on physical relationships and the naïve idealisms of romantic love. The contrast with the earlier poems, however, is instructive. The later poems have a depth and complexity, in large part a result of the allusions used in them, which is lacking in the earlier ones. The scatological poems are the more interesting and significant, despite the difficulties Swift had with subject and tone.[21]

Those difficulties are epitomized by the contrast between Ovid's light, dispassionate comedy and the heavier, more intense tone that slips into Swift's. Ovid approves of passion generally and urges those who have delight in their love to "rejoice and sail on"; neither in theme nor tone does Swift ever convey such approval. Ovid accepts and uses the physical: satiety with, or distaste after, coition is a principal "remedy" for excess passion. Swift shows no such tolerance: coition is replaced in his poems by excrement or ugliness, and Swift himself is in some degree offended by what he satirizes his characters for being offended by.[22] Recent criticism has been very valuable in demonstrating that Swift was neither mad nor utterly misanthropic in the scatological poems[23]; but it has created a new misunderstanding by assuming that Swift was totally consistent in his feelings and art, using scatology skillfully as a satiric or moralistic weapon.[24] The difficulties and inconsistencies in the scatological poems are real and must be recognized. Yet, paradoxically, they are also a part of the poems' fascination and power. It is precisely our impression of disgust erupting through the effort to cloak it in humor, our impression of loss of control by a man who is trying to exhibit his self-control, that makes these poems compelling despite their often disagreeable images and tones.

A common conviction, then, runs through all Swift's poems about women. The satiric poems attacking women as well as the straightforward poems praising Stella assert that in human relationships the internal must be preferred over the external, reason over passion, friendship over romance. Yet the methods through which this theme is developed differ considerably, and those differences trace the course of Swift's growth as a poet. "To Lord Harley" uses allusions to convey its theme with depth and subtlety, an evidence of the skill and sophistication Swift attained as a poet by 1715. The "Progress" poems and the poems to Stella, with their paucity of allusions and their resulting directness and didacticism, are typical of the poems of the decade following 1715, when Swift was not giving his primary attention to poetry and was not growing as a poet. It is only late in the 1720s that the earlier techniques reappear and develop further. The scatological poems, using allusions freely, if not always well, to affect tone and shape meaning, anticipate the great political satires of the 1730s, with their powerful integration of allusions and form.

V

Neither So Ill a Subject Nor So Stupid an Author
Poems Personal and Political

Perhaps it was because Swift's strategy for using allusions originated with the classical imitation that classical works continued to be an important source of allusions throughout his career. As the previous three chapters have shown, the classics provided key allusions in the early satires, the personal poems, and the scatological poems. In a group of poems beginning in the late 1720s, however, Swift experimented with a type of allusion different from the literary references of the earlier poems. Having discovered that allusions could enable him to make poems function simultaneously on two or more levels, Swift used images and catchwords from contemporary pamphlets and journals to work a complementary political theme into a series of later personal poems. The poems examined in this chapter—"Verses on the Death of Dr. Swift," the Delany poems, "An Epistle to a Lady," and "On Poetry: A Rapsody"—cannot be fully under-

stood or appreciated, individually or as a group, without attention to the context supplied by political writings of the day.

I

Consideration of these poems as personal poems must begin
with Swift's prose apologias, earlier and less ambiguous than the
verse apologias of the late 1720s and early 1730s. The clearest
example is Swift's "letter" to Pope of 10 January 1720/21.[1] It
begins as if its emphasis will be defense of Swift as an author.
Swift first mentions three of his writings—"Some Free Thoughts
upon the Present State of Affairs," some memorials he is writing
upon the last four years of the queen's reign, and a discourse to
persuade the wretched people of Ireland to wear their own manufactures instead of those from England. But he spends little
time on the works themselves, concentrating instead on their
results: the letter dwells in detail on a difference in opinion with
a great minister that prevented publication of "Some Free Thoughts,"
on the appointment to the office of historiographer required for
completion of the memorials, and on the prosecution of Edward
Waters the printer that resulted from publication of the "discourse." Swift is not so much defending his works as expressing
indignation that his principles, motives, and abilities could be
so mistaken or misrepresented as to produce such effects. He
notes emphatically that "the Chief Justice, among other singu-
larities, laid his hand on his breast, and protested solemnly that
the Author's design was to bring in the Pretender; although
there was not a single syllable of Party in the whole Treatise"
(p. 27). The only other reference to his writings is to deny author-
ship of "some writings . . . of which any man of common sense
and literature would be heartily ashamed" (p. 28). Again, the
affront is personal: although he expresses concern for the insipidity
of those works and the ill "taste for wit and sense" which prevails
in the world (p. 27), the chief source of his indignation seems to

be that his abilities are not sufficiently well known and respected
to prevent such incorrect ascriptions.

Most of the letter is spent defending his values and principles,
showing further his concern for the person behind the writings.
He was of some importance in the Oxford-Bolingbroke ministry;
he did his best to reconcile the ministers to each other and would
have succeeded if others had done their parts; he was not parti-
san in his service to the ministry, but chose his friends and
recommended people for positions "by their personal merit,
without examining how far their notions agreed with the politicks then in vogue" (p. 29). What he did and stood for, however,
have probably been ignored or perhaps forgotten, and "with
great injustice I have these many years been pelted by your Pam-
phleteers" (p. 30). "*I was known*," he goes on indignantly, "to be
a common Friend of all deserving persons" (p. 30; italics added),
but that is no longer being remembered or appreciated. Because
so much is being overlooked or forgotten, he spells out in detail,
in the last section of the letter, the "old whiggish principles" (p.
33) he held and holds and wants to be known for: acceptance of
the Protestant line and the Revolution of 1688, opposition to
standing armies, preference for annual Parliaments, and support
for landed over monied interests. The principles are those of a
man deeply committed to personal liberty, a man to be trusted
and respected, a man who could be expected to produce only
works of high merit in "Style or Sentiments" (p. 25). In such a
spirit he summarizes his defense: "All I can reasonably hope for
by this letter, is to convince my friends and others who are pleased
to wish me well, that I have neither been so ill a Subject nor so
stupid an Author, as I have been represented by the virulence of
Libellers, whose malice hath taken the same train in both, by
fathering dangerous principles in government upon me, which I
never maintained, and insipid productions which I am not
capable of writing" (pp. 33–34). It is not merely, or even chiefly,
a defense of himself as a writer. The emphasis is on Swift as a
man of importance and of principle, and as a man misrepresented
and maligned on both accounts.

Swift's later prose apologias follow much the same pattern, in tone and topics. The next one appeared several years later, during an encounter with Archbishop King.[2] King had demanded—contrary to usual practices, Swift emphasizes—a proxy in view of Swift's absence from the archbishop's visitation of his chapter. Swift insists (1) that the archbishop has always opposed Swift because of their political differences, an opposition all the more unjust because "during some years when I was thought to have credit with those in power, I employed it to the utmost for your service" (p. 210), even though King was a Whig, and (2) that, having always been "an enemy to servitude and slavery of all kinds," especially in Ireland, he thinks, and has been told, "I deserved better from that Church and that kingdom," and many will attest "that all my merits are not very old" (pp. 210–11). Again there is a deep sense of injury because his efforts and achievements for others are not being remembered and recognized. And this seems to concern him the more because "I have not long to live" (p. 211).

A series of references to death and brief apologetic passages begins about this time in the correspondence,[3] culminating in two letters in 1729, about the time the later series of personal poems begins. In a letter to Pope (5 April 1729) Swift makes an unusually frank and nonironic admission about his motives and values: "All my endeavours from a boy to distinguish my self, were only for want of a great Title and Fortune, that I might be used like a Lord by those who have an opinion of my parts; . . . and so the reputation of wit or great learning does the office of a blue riband, or of a coach and six horses. . . . I never loved to make a visit, or be seen walking with my betters, because they get all the eyes and civilities from me" (*Corres.*, III, 330–31). The same need for recognition and acceptance by those he looks up to appears as he elaborates on this thought in a letter to Bolingbroke a few months later (31 October 1729): "Because I cannot be a great Lord, I would acquire what is a kind of Subsidium, I would endeavour that my betters shall seek me by the merit of something distinguishable instead of my seeking them" (*Corres.*, III, 355). The "something distinguishable" could be—and surely to some degree was—repute as an author. But his artistic works are rarely mentioned or defended in his apologias. Perhaps literary "fame, like all things else in this life," really did grow with him "every day more a trifle" (*Corres.*, III, 330). More likely, he could take the attitude that his literary works have an independent existence: they will remain, and what he says in their defense can make little difference, just as the "Apology" for *A Tale of a Tub* had no effect on Queen Anne or others predisposed against the work.

But what he was and what he did as a person had no such external embodiment, although they were just as important to him, if not more so. For that reason the friendship and regard of men such as Oxford, Bolingbroke, and Pope always were important, and became even more important as the end of his life approached. He urges Pope, several times, "*Orna me*" [adorn, or honor, me];[4] he remembers "in one of your Letters you s^d you intended that an Epistle should be inscribed to me";[5] and he dislikes Pope's continued work on the *Dunciad Variorum* "because it defers gratifying my vanity in the most tender point, and perhaps may wholly disappoint it."[6] Such relationships not only indicate his worth at the present, but will confirm it in the future. Thus it is not entirely tongue-in-cheek when he assures Pope and Bolingbroke that "to be remembred for ever on the account of our friendship, is what would exceedingly please me," and when he tells Gay, "If I am your friend it is for my own reputation, and from a principle of Self-love,"[7] and when he writes of Orrery and Delany,

> And let the friendly Lines they writ
> In praise of long departed Wit,
> Be grav'd on either Side [of my Tomb] in Columns,
> More to my Praise than all my Volumes.[8]

His desire is to be recognized now and later as a worthy associate, friend, and confidant of the greatest writers and statesmen of his age. And it is on that ground that he becomes so distressed over, and attempts to reply to, the forgetfulness, ingratitude, and disparagement he encounters throughout his career.

Such disparagement led to "The Substance of What was said by the Dean of St. Patricks to the Lord Mayor and some of the Aldermen, when his Lordship came to present the said Dean with his Freedom in a Gold Box."[9] Because Lord Allen protested against the award, Swift prepared this overt defense of himself and his deeds: "The Dean further said, That, since he had been so falsely represented, he thought it became him to give some account of himself for above twenty years, if it were only to justify his Lordship and the city for the honour they were going to do him" (pp. 146–47). He lists six areas which justify the honor, besides "several other particulars": (1) "he had procured a grant of the first fruits to the clergy, in the late Queen's time"; (2) he had been "a constant advocate for those who are called the Whigs"; (3) he was treated severely by the Whigs in the years after her Majesty's death; (4) he had lent money "without interest, in small sums to poor industrious tradesmen" and thus "recovered above two hundred families in this city from ruin"; (5) he was persecuted by "a most iniquitous judge; who . . . had condemned an innocent book"; and (6) he "freely confessed himself to be author of those books called the *Drapier's Letters*" (p. 147). The emphasis is on what he accomplished (nos. 1, 4, 6—for the Drapier's Letters are surely being valued for their effect rather than for their artistry) and on efforts to disparage or deny his accomplishments (persecution by the Whigs rankles most because it ignores *what he had done* for the Whigs). He concludes with an explicit desire to have his accomplishments given an enduring form: "The Dean concluded with acknowledging to have expressed his wishes, that an inscription might have been graven on the box, shewing some reason why the city thought fit to do him that honour, which was much out of the common forms to a person in a private station" (p. 148). That

desire for a permanent record of what he was and did sums up
the purposes of his apologias in prose and in verse also, as can
best be illustrated by "Verses on the Death of Dr. Swift."

"Verses on the Death of Dr. Swift" continues Swift's concern
with being ignored, unrecognized, and forgotten, and supplies
the theory which accounts for it. The poem develops a thought
of La Rochefoucauld, printed in French and English as epigraph—"Dan l'adversité de nos meilleurs amis nous trouvons
quelque chose, qui ne nous deplaist pas—In the Adversity of our
best Friends, we find something that doth not displease us"—
and rephrased as follows in the poem:

> "In all Distresses of our Friends
> "We first consult our private Ends,
> "While Nature kindly bent to ease us,
> "Points out some Circumstance to please us.
> (7–10)

The poem "proves" this maxim by "Reason" in the "Proem"
(13–72), and by "Experience" in the "Poem" (73–484), specifically
by the circumstances before (73–146), at the time of (147–242),
and a year after (243–484) Swift's own death. The same impulse
that makes a man want to "Stand high himself, keep others
low" (16) also prompts him to ignore or forget persons and deeds
which deserve to be recognized and praised.

> What Poet would not grieve to see,
> His Brethren write as well as he?
> But rather than they should excel,
> He'd wish his Rivals all in Hell.
> (31–34)

For friends or foes, "private Ends" (76) are placed ahead of due
credit or praise. Before Swift's death, in the specific example he
provides, his "special Friends" (75) ignore his earlier achievements and concern themselves only with his sickly state, for
that affords them the greater satisfaction that " 'It is not yet so
bad with us" (116). At the Dean's death, other selfish attitudes

become clear: the queen's lack of appreciation—" 'I'm glad the
Medals were forgot" (184); Walpole's lack of fear—" 'Oh, were
the Wretch but living still, / And in his Place my good Friend
Will" (193–94); and Curll's lack of respect, as he lists the Dean's
literary remains as "Revis'd by *Tibbalds, Moore, and Cibber*"
(200). Even "those I love"—note that he avoids claiming that
they love him or that others will remember them as his friends—
will forget him quickly:

> Poor POPE will grieve a Month; and GAY
> A Week; and ARBUTHNOTT a Day.
> (207–8)

A year after his death Dr. Swift and his achievements are completely forgotten:

> No further mention of the Dean;
> Who now, alas, no more is mist,
> Than if he never did exist.
> (246–48)

Throughout all this there is obvious exaggeration, but beneath
the hyperbole lies a truth that haunted Swift and that impelled
him to write the apologias in prose and verse.

"Verses on the Death of Dr. Swift," then, is another attempt
to preserve for posterity a sense of who Swift was and what he
achieved. As in the prose apologias, there is little emphasis on
his literary works: although " 'The Dean was famous in his
Time," " 'His way of Writing now is past" (263, 265). The defense will be, rather, of his life and works. Swift has been accused
of egotism and indefensibly bad judgment in the "Verses";[10]
such a charge stems from a misunderstanding of the strategy of
the poem. The main apologia is carried out in the footnotes,
with the first half of the poem presenting the need for such an
apologia and the latter half carrying out a political attack better
discussed later in this chapter.

Therefore, it is to the footnotes, generally more temperate and
factual than the poem itself, that one must look for Swift's de-

fense of himself. Apart from a few which merely convey information, the footnotes read like a condensation of the prose
apologias summarized above. The first footnote provides the
apologetic framework: "The Author imagines"—no persona or
irony, just Swift defending himself with an explicit goal in mind—
"that . . . others will remember him with Gratitude," especially
for his achievements "under the Name of M. B. Drapier." After
two notes on the ingratitude of the queen for his gift of "a Piece
of *Indian* Plad made in [Ireland]," there are three notes on Walpole, Bolingbroke, and Pulteney, which, like the lines in the
poem mentioning his literary friends (47–66), emphasize his
associations with the great. The note on Walpole, significantly,
stresses the latter's civilities to Swift: whatever his politics (and
they will be provided for later), the Great Man knew and respected Swift. Next are two notes on Curll, who "published
three Volumes all charged on the Dean, who never writ three
Pages of them." When literature is mentioned, it is, as in the
earlier apologias, with annoyance that people did not immediately realize he could not possibly have written such works as
have been foisted on him. Then comes a series of notes listing
achievements of the Dean, many with rhetorical twists designed
to prove his value and success. The rewards of three hundred
pounds which were twice placed on his head are convincing
proof of his strength as a pamphleteer and Patriot, and the
"Hundreds of Libels writ against him in *England*" witness to his
eminence and effectiveness as a political writer during the queen's
last years. Likewise, that "all the Kingdom took the *Drapier's*
Part" may be forgotten or disputed, but that "his Sign was set
up in most Streets of *Dublin* (where many of them still continue)
and in several Country Towns" cannot be denied or discounted.
This apologia, testifying to Swift's effectiveness and importance,
is very different from Pope's, for it arises out of very different
needs and purposes. Pope, after all, lived for and through his
literature; thus, to justify his satires would be to justify himself
as a person. Swift, on the other hand, thrived on social and

political status: his years in London during the Tory ministry and his accomplishments as the Drapier were the high points of his life, what he wanted to be remembered and praised for. To justify himself as a person, therefore, would be to justify his writings as well. The emphasis in the apologias, in prose and in verse, is on who Swift was, what he stood for, and what he accomplished—or, in other words, on those endeavors to distinguish himself for "want of a great Title and Fortune."

II

The "Verses" and other personal poems of the late 1720s and the early 1730s are in part apologia—but they are more than that. Swift had another deep interest and concern at the time. In May 1727 he wrote back from London to Thomas Sheridan that "we are here in a strange Situation; a firm, settled Resolution to assault the present Administration, and break it if possible" (*Corres.*, III, 207). He counted himself an integral part of the Opposition during his stay in London, as the pronouns in this letter to Sheridan, two months later, indicate: "We have now done with Repining, if we shall be used well, and not baited as formerly; we all agree in it, and if Things do not mend it is not our Faults: We have made our Offers: If otherwise, we are as we were."[11] Upon his return to Ireland he continued to be informed about the English situation[12] and hopeful that a change was imminent: "We are taught to hope here, that Events may happen in no long time, which may give the Court another face with reguard to you as well as all wellwishers to their Country."[13] Shortly thereafter he shows concern about the Opposition's success: "But I have other difficultyes besides my private affairs to detain me: No offence to Your Lordship, I am not very fond of the publick Scituation. I see nails that I thought might be pulled out, now more strongly riveted than ever."[14] And a year later he rejoices in the unanimity Walpole's policies are creating among his opponents: "It is a great comfort to See how corruption and ill conduct are instrumental in uniting Virtuous Persons and lovers of their country of all denominations Lord B[olingbroke] with W[illiam] P[ulteney] Sir W[illiam] W[yndham] with the [Duke and Duchess of Queensbury]."[15]

That interest in Opposition efforts carries over into the poems. When he wrote "Directions for a Birth-day Song" (1729), Swift reflected the optimistic assumption of the moment that Walpole was vulnerable:

> To Walpole you might lend a Line,
> But much I fear he's in decline.
> (255–56)

A year or two later, that optimism behind him, he unleashes a venomous assault in "The Character of Sir Robert Walpole" (1731):

> With favour & fortune fastidiously blest
> he's loud in his laugh & he's coarse in his Jest.
> (1–2)

References in "To Mr. Gay" (1731) are equally harsh:

> A bloated M[iniste]r in all his Geer,
> With shameless Visage, and perfidious Leer.
>
> .   .   .   .
>
> Of loud un-meaning Sounds, a rapid Flood
> Rolls from his Mouth in plenteous Streams of Mud;
> With these, the Court and Senate-house he plies,
> Made up of Noise, and Impudence, and Lies.
> (33–42)

These poems—in which Swift mingles defense of himself with attacks on Walpole, condemnation of flattery, and praise of his friends—are unified by their allusions to the libel-panegyric theme that runs throughout the attacks the Opposition was directing at the Walpole ministry in various papers and pamphlets at the time, especially in *The Craftsman.*

The Craftsman, the most interesting and imaginative of the many journals of the 1720s and '30s, is characterized by a number of clearly identifiable themes which give it unity and reflect the various strategies of the Opposition. The early numbers tend toward varied, wide-ranging attacks on corruption in many forms, but especially the enlargement of office, enrichment, and bribery resulting from Walpole's rule.[16] The attacks are largely personal, reflecting the Opposition's hope of discrediting Walpole and driving him from office. The most dominant motif in these years of personal attack, from 1721 to 1731, is that of panegyric and libel (afterward, it disappears almost entirely, as the Opposition shifts to an attack on the basis of issues instead of personalities). The motif was based on Walpole's practice of hiring hack writers to defend his policies: "He was an Enemy to *polite Learning*," writes *The Craftsman*, "and bestow'd all his Favours on a Parcel of *paltry Scribblers*, whom He retain'd in his Service."[17] From such practices, it was an easy step to assume that those writers would praise not only policies but the policymaker as well, and that that indeed was precisely the intention. The first issue of *The Occasional Writer* affects to have a hack writer appealing to Walpole for support: "Employ me, Sir, as you please, I abandon my self intirely to you, my Pen is at your disposition, and my conscience in your keeping. . . . I cancel at once all former obligations and friendships, and will most implicitly follow your instructions in Panegyrick on your self and friends, in Satyr on your adversaries, in writing for or against any subject."[18] The writers for *The Craftsman* seized on this as a favorite attack. *Craftsman* Number 90, for example, includes "A Panegyrical Address to a certain great Man," which imitates the "flowing Style and forcible Manner" of "a State Panegyrist."[19] Another *Craftsman* reviews a "late emblematical Panegyrick to the Glory of a certain great Man."[20] Two recurring satiric devices in the early numbers of *The Craftsman* grow directly out of this. One is various comparisons of Walpole to Cardinal Wolsey, as, for example, a poem entitled "A Panegyrick *on Cardinal W——*."[21] The other is adaptation of the mock advertisements which *The*

Craftsman frequently included. The following appeared in Number 55:

ADVERTISEMENT.

This Week was publish'd,
ROBIN's *Panegyrick on* Himself *and his Friends at* Westminister; *modestly proving that they are all very* honest Fellows *and* deserving Patriots; *with a full Confutation of the Charge of* Bribery *and* Corruption.[22]

And in Number 94 appears the advertisement for "Robin's Panegyrick on Himself and his Coadjutors at Westminister. Part the Second. . . . To be continued, as Occasion requires."[23] But satire on the ministry's panegyrics is not restricted to *The Craftsman.* James Bramston, in *The Art of Politicks*, gives the following advice:

> Ye *Weekly Writers* of seditious *News,*
> Take Care your *Subjects* artfully to chuse,
> Write *Panegyrick* strong, or boldly *rail,*
> You cannot miss *Preferment*, or a *Goal*.[24]

And it is reflected once more in the title of a miscellany published in three parts (1729, 1731, 1733): *Robin's Panegyrick; or, The Norfolk Miscellany.*[25]

From 1731 on panegyric disappears from *The Craftsman*, and the word is rarely even used. By then it was obvious that Walpole would not be shaken by personal vendettas, and the attempt to unseat him shifts to attacks based upon issues. After 1731, the decline of old English values, especially freedom, the dangers inherent in standing armies, the excise, and the "Liberty of the Press" to publish writings opposing the ministry become the recurrent themes. References in *The Craftsman* to the writings of its opponents as "libels" abound from the beginning, and appear just as often in the writings of the opponents. Thus, Sir William Yonge attacked *The Craftsman* for its "Libels, [which] are no *Satires*," and William Pulteney replied with his *Answer to One Part of a late Infamous Libel*.[26] But *The Craftsman* goes on to accuse the ministry of attempting to suppress opposition attacks

by calling them "libels" and, in so doing, gives "libel" as much
emphasis and importance as "panegyrick." As *The Craftsman*
itself puts it, "Every Thing is a *Libel*, which Men in Authority
may think fit to call so, however *dark* or *obscure* or *innocent* it
may be."[27] From libel *The Craftsman* moves to the broader issue
of liberty: "We know very well, by Experience, how far our *Adversaries* are willing to allow the *Liberty of Writing*, and to what
Bounds they would restrain the Use of it; That is, to Panegyricks
and Encomiums on all *ministerial Schemes.*"[28] Sir William Yonge,
defending the ministry in *Sedition and Defamation Display'd*,
acknowledges the charge by describing it as a "Noble Expedient,"
which includes, "First, to write and publish seditious and trai-
terous Libels against the Government, and His Majesty himself,
which must necessarily draw down a *just* and *legal* Prosecution
of the Authors and Publishers; and then to complain of that
just and necessary Prosecution, as an Infringement of the *Liberty
of the Press*, and the Right of every *Englishman*" (p. 20). Panegyric
and libel, often used separately, are also frequently combined,
imaginatively and effectively, by writers for *The Craftsman*:
"There is no great Quality, for which *some Gentlemen* have been
more celebrated by their *Advocates and Encomiasts in ordinary*,
than That of *Lenity* and *Forbearance* towards Those, who are
call'd *Libellers*. . . . This Topick hath constantly made a Part of
their Panegyricks."[29]

Here then are the two sides of an enduring and important
strategy of attack, with which anyone close to the Opposition—
including Swift—would have been familiar in the late 1720s and
early 1730s.

III

It can hardly be coincidental, therefore, that a libel-panegyric
motif, applied specifically to political targets, appears in Swift's
verse satires from 1729 through 1734. The motif first appears in
"Directions for a Birth-day Song" (1729), a piece of ironic advice

to hack poets on how to write panegyrics to the royal family. But it runs more strongly through the Delany poems. This series of poems began when Swift's friend Patrick Delany wrote a poem to Lord Carteret praising Carteret profusely and requesting some evidence of Carteret's "Favour." Swift twitted Delany for his fulsomeness in "An Epistle upon an Epistle" (January 1730), comparing Delany to Swift's old enemy the Duke of Grafton and admonishing Delany to "Be Modest: nor Address your Betters / With Begging, Vain, Familiar Letters" (117–18). But Swift saw more serious implications in Delany's action and, in that year, followed up with a series of three poems that focus on libel and panegyric.

The first, "A Libel on D—— D——. And a Certain Great Lord," was published in February 1730. It deserves attention, if for no other reason, because of Swift's comment in a letter to Benjamin Motte that it is "the best thing I writt as I think" (4 November 1732, *Corres.*, IV, 83). He valued it so highly, I suspect, not only because it is a lively, wide-ranging, and hard-hitting satire, but also because it combines in one poem the three topics he seems most concerned with at the time: praise of his friends, defense of himself, and sharp, satiric attack on Walpole and the Whig ministry. These three topics are unified by the poem's use of libel and panegyric. Swift first attacks patronage and the stooping (like Delany's to Carteret) required for poets' survival. Thus, his friend Congreve was penniless "Till Prudence taught him to appeal / From *Paean's* Fire to *Party* Zeal" (43–44). Gay and Addison likewise were forced into compromises by a system whose corruption is evinced by its craving for praise:

> For, as their Appetites to quench,
> Lords keep a Pimp to bring a Wench;
> So, Men of Wit are but a kind
> Of Pandars to a vicious Mind,
> Who proper Objects must provide
> To gratify their Lust of Pride.
>   (21–26)

Only Pope is credited with having totally escaped such a fate: "His Heart too Great, though Fortune little, / To lick a *Rascal Stateman's* Spittle" (81–82). Delany did not escape it. In order to get preferment, Delany had to become a "Sweet'ner" (154), praising Carteret while overlooking the fact that Carteret came to Ireland as Walpole's agent:

> He comes to *drain* a *Beggar's Purse:*
> He comes to tye our Chains on faster,
> And shew us, E[ngland] is our Master.
>   (124–26)

Much as he respects and likes Carteret, however, Swift will not flatter him:

> I own, he hates an Action base,
> His *Virtues* battling with his *Place*;
> Nor wants a nice discerning Spirit,
> Betwixt a true and spurious Merit;
> Can sometimes drop a *Voter's* Claim,
> And give up Party to his Fame.
> I do the most that *Friendship* can;
> I hate the *Vice-Roy*, love the Man.
>   (145–52)

Nor will he back away from describing accurately Carteret's role and effect in Ireland. A flatterer would excuse Carteret as follows:

> "So, to destroy a guilty Land,
> "An *Angel* sent by *Heav'n's* Command,
> "While he obeys *Almighty* Will,
> "Perhaps, may feel *Compassion* still,
> "And wish the Task had been assign'd
> "To *Spirits* of less gentle kind.
>   (165–70)

But Swift, getting his words "Fresh from the *Tripod* of Apollo" (181), proposes "an Allusion fitter" (177) which "Would shew you many a *Statesman*'s Face" (180):

> So, to effect his M[onarc]h's ends,
> From *Hell* a V[iceroy] DEV'L ascends,
> His *Budget* with *Corruptions* cramm'd,
> The Contributions of the *damn'd*;
> Which with unsparing Hand, he strows
> Through *Courts* and *Senates* as he goes;
> And then at *Beelzebub*'s *Black-Hall*,
> Complains his *Budget* was too small.
>   (185–92)

The standard which a poet must set himself is truth:

> Your *Simile* may better shine
> In Verse; but there is *Truth* in mine.
>   (193–94)

Instead of exposing evil, the poet who flatters endorses it and makes it attractive and deceptive by cloaking it in the beauty of art. Against such corruption and such encouragement of it, Swift uses himself as a positive illustration:

> But I, in *Politicks* grown old,
> Whose Thoughts are of a diff'rent Mold,
> Who, from my Soul, sincerely hate
> Both [Kings] and *Ministers* of *State*,
> Who look on *Courts* with stricter Eyes,
> To see the Seeds of *Vice* arise.
>   (171–76)

It is less an assertion of himself as a person, however, than as a clear-sighted seeker of truth, and it is confirmed by example: the attacks on the court and ministry throughout the poem are the firmest evidence that he will say what he must. At the heart of the poem and of the libel-panegyric motif is the responsibility of the poet: the poet must, somehow, stay free of patronage because it is his duty not to flatter, but to say the truth and even to "libel" when he must.

A month or two after writing a "libel" to Delany, Swift wrote a "panegyric" in answer to it—"A Panegyric on the Reverend D——n S——t In Answer to the Libel on Dr. D——y, and a certain Great L——d"—with Delany as "author." This poem is much less serious in tone and theme than the "Libel," as it parodies the "style and manner" of the hack poets Swift has been attacking. The focus of the poem, as well as the serious point it does make, again involves the mixing of panegyric and politics, though the emphasis is more specifically on advancement, as befits a poem "written" by Delany. Delany, turning words from the "Libel" against Swift, accuses him of various time-serving measures—"But form'd more perfect *Gamester*, you / The deepest *Tricks* of *Courtiers* knew" (37–38)—and of gaining advancement through flattery:

> No Wonder you should think it *little*
> To *lick a Rascal Statesman's Spittle*,
> Who have, to shew your great Devotion,
> Oft' swallow'd down a stronger Potion,
> A Composition more absurd,
> *Bob's Spittle*, mix'd with *Harry's* T——.
> (58–63)

Although the mock-panegyric attacks Swift for many such faults, Swift noted in a letter to Bathurst in October 1730 that "I took special care to accuse myself but of one fault of which I am really guilty" (*Corres.*, III, 410). Williams, in his edition of the *Poems* (II, 493n), identifies that reference as in lines 17–20:

> Where'er the Wind of *Favour* sits,
> It still your Constitution hits.
> If fair, it brings you safe to Port,
> And when 'tis foul, affords you Sport.

But Swift surely did not mean that the one fault of which he was really guilty was that of taking advantage of "the Wind of *Favour*" to gain his "*Deanery*" (21). He felt deeply that he was qualified for the position he received and, indeed, for a higher and better

one. In his edition of the *Correspondence*, Williams, even more
unaccountably, suggests that the fault of which Swift was really
guilty was being "deficient in wit,"[30] citing these lines as evidence:

> You never had commenc'd a *Dean*,
> Unless you other Ways had trod
> Than those of *Wit*, or Trust in GOD.
>   (77–79)

But surely these lines, too, are ironic: Swift believed sincerely
that his abilities and beliefs had merited a deanship, while his
failure to pursue "other Ways" prevented him from receiving a
higher post. The fault of which Swift really was guilty comes in
some lines concerning an issue more pertinent to Swift at the
time, events surrounding "the Gift / Of our *Metropolis* to S——*t*"
(47–48):

> The Gift (good Heav'ns preserve't from Thieves)
> Of *Lord-May'r*, *Aldermen*, and *Shrieves*,
> Where, if the curious List to read 'em,
> They'll find his Life, and Acts, and *Freedom*,
> And the great Name engrav'd most fairly,
> Of him that *Ireland* sav'd, and *Harley*.
>   (49–54)

Swift took justifiable pride in receiving an "honour, which was
much out of the common forms to a person in a private station."[31] His pleasure in the occasion was lessened, however, by
the way Lord Allen attacked him: "This same Allin about a
fortnight ago, at the Privy Council . . . reproached the City for
their resolution of giving me my freedom in a Goldbox, calling
me a Jacobite Libeller &c. and hath now brought the same affair into the H. of Lords."[32] Yet that same Lord Allen and his
Lady had been "some years caressing me in the most friendly
manner,"[33] illustrating yet again the emptiness of flattery. The
fault of which Swift was really guilty, then, was that of saving
Ireland, and it is that to which he refers as his letter to Bathurst
goes on: "And so [I] shall continue [in that 'fault'] as I have done

these 16 years till I see cause to reform." Here again panegyric—both the flattery of Lord and Lady Allen and the praise Delany supposedly wrote on the Reverend Dean Swift—is empty, unreliable, deceptive. The praise which is of value, solid recognition awarded by an entire community, is for what he has *done*—for a series of ironic essays important, not for their beauty, but for their effect, for their revelation of the truth about some brass coins and the political and economic status of Ireland.

In the third Delany poem, "To Doctor D—L——Y, on the Libels Writ against him," late in 1730, Swift defines in broadest terms the effects of the combining of panegyric and politics. Those subjected to "stupid Libels" (43), the poet tells Delany, have two remedies available to them. One is to stop writing: "Lye down obscure like other Folks / Below the Lash of Snarlers Jokes" (45–46). The other, for those who find that they must write, is to turn party writer and "The *Irish Senate's* Praises sing" (56). References to such political scribblers give Swift an excuse to level an attack at Walpole and, beyond him, at the party he represents:

> Aspiring, factious, fierce and loud
> With Grace and Learning unendow'd,
> Can turn their Hands to ev'ry Jobb,
> The fittest Tools to work for *Bobb*.
> Will sooner coyn a Thousand Lyes
> Than suffer Men of Parts to rise.
>
> (87–92)

The party scribblers on the one hand libel the good writers, the "Men of Parts," and thus make their ascendence more difficult; and on the other hand, they flatter a party and its politicians who utterly do not merit it and endorse policies which ought to be condemned and resisted. A political party steeped in corruption, using and working in collusion with literary figures, has created a corrupt and decadent social condition which the clearsighted, the nonflatterers, like Swift, must expose and attack.

> Wit, as the chief of Virtue's Friends,
> Disdains to serve ignoble Ends.
> Observe what Loads of stupid Rimes
> Oppress us in corrupted Times:
> What Pamphlets in a Court's Defence
> Shew Reason, Grammer, Truth, or Sense?
> (99–104)

Swift, it seems clear, sees himself as an exemplar of reason, grammar, and sense in the cause of truth and virtue. For that he expects to be attacked: "Dame Nature as the Learned show, / Provides each Animal it's Foe" (127–28); but though his foes will libel him, "Praise bestow'd in Grub-Street Rimes, / Would vex one more a thousand Times" (165–66). Swift recommends to Delany the attitude he himself takes:

> On me, when Dunces are satyrick,
> I take it for a Panegyrick.
> *Hated by Fools*, and *Fools to hate*,
> Be that my Motto, and my Fate.
> (169–72)

Only by opposing bad poets can a good poet be assured he is adequately doing his job, for he is then opposing the social and political decline of which the bad poet is the clearest evidence.

IV

"Verses on the Death of Dr. Swift" is also, in large part, a political poem, attacking the same social evils and political leaders as the Delany poems, reflecting the same pattern of panegyric and libel. Neglect of this major theme has been one reason for the wide diversity of readings the poem has received.[34] In the "Verses," as in the Delany poems, the full meaning evolves from an interaction of the personal with the political.

Although the political emphasis appears in passing several times in the first half of the poem, it is most important in the

second half, the "eulogy" on Swift. A brief outline of the eulogy
will clarify its content:

307–70:   general praise of Swift
371–90:   survey of the political situation in 1713–14
391–406: Swift's exile and oppression in Ireland
407–30:   Swift's role in the Wood affair
431–54:   Swift's opposition to the Irish Parliament
455–84:   general praise of Swift

The first point one might observe in considering this outline is
the lack of emphasis on what Swift *did*. The emphasis in Swift's
straightforward apologias, as we have seen, is on his accomplishments; the fact that the eulogy emphasizes what Swift suffered
suggests that its main purpose is not apologetic. A second point
to be observed about the outline is that one issue runs throughout: the Whig party and corruptions associated with it. The
section which surveys politics in 1713–14 comes to focus on the
takeover by a "dangerous Faction . . . / With Wrath and Vengeance in their Hearts" (379–80). The section on Swift's exile in
Ireland emphasizes his "continual Persecution" (400) by the
Whigs, who were also persecuting Oxford and Bolingbroke. In
the next section, the reference to those "who at the Steerage
stood" (413) during the time William Wood was pressing his
coins upon the Irish directs one's attention past Wood to the
Whigs and particularly to Walpole, "who was said," writes the
Drapier, "to have sworn some Months ago, that he woud *ram
them down our Throats.*"[35] And the conduct of Chief Justice Whit-
shed, the "wicked Monster on the Bench" (417) in the trials of
Edward Waters and John Harding, was motivated—the Dean
later told the lord mayor and the aldermen when they came to
present his Freedom in a Gold Box—by "ambition and rage of
party" (*Prose Works*, XII, 147). Finally, the Parliament in Ireland,
which Swift attacks here and elsewhere, was "by its constitution
and composition . . . almost wholly subservient to English [and
thus Whig] influence or control."[36] One purpose of the eulogy,

then, in common with the other poems of this period, is an attack on the Whigs in general and Walpole in particular.

To understand the further purposes of the eulogy and its relationship to the first half of the poem requires attention to the character who delivers the eulogy. Critics have tended to view that character either as Swift's alter ego or as an ironic mask; rarely has he been considered as a character set in a dramatic situation. Yet the first half of the poem is built of conversations or speeches of characters whose distinctness is not questioned: "My special Friends" (73–134), "My good Companions" (143–64), the doctors (169–76), Lady Suffolk and the queen (179–88), Walpole (189–96), Lintot (255–98), and of course "My female Friends" (225–42). When Swift deliberately separates the eulogist from himself—"One quite indiff'rent in the Cause, / My Character impartial draws" (305–6)—it seems at least possible that this is an extension of the method established and used throughout the first half of the poem to illustrate dramatically and concretely the self-interest of various characters on the occasion of Swift's death. When Swift has that character deliver his eulogy in the Rose Tavern, which was consistently used in the Restoration and early eighteenth century as a symbol of disrepute,[37] he further emphasizes the dramatic situation and provides the first grounds for suspicion about the eulogist.

Swift's assurance that the eulogist was "indiff'rent in the Cause" provides further ground for suspicion about him. It should make readers as wary as they would be of the soldiers mentioned by the historian in *The Battle of the Books*, in which men from both sides of a battle set up trophies and inscribe on them "the Merits of the Cause; a full impartial Account of . . . how the Victory fell clearly to the Party that set them up."[38] The ironic exaggerations of Swift's merits as a writer confirm the eulogist's lack of indifference and objectivity in regard to Swift: " 'But what he writ was all his own" (318) and " 'He lash'd the Vice but spar'd the Name" (460). Such exaggerated claims about Swift's writings are matched by equally inflated and ironic claims about Swift's personal life:

"Though trusted long in great Affairs,
"He gave himself no haughty Airs.

(329–30)

"But, Power was never in his Thought;
"And, Wealth he valu'd not a Groat.

(357–58)

"Was chearful to his dying Day.

(477)

The eulogist is not, by any means, an impartial reporter. He is selective about the details of Swift's life he includes, he hyperbolizes those he does include, and he shows a definite preoccupation with politics throughout. Out of his choices and emphases, his character, as much of it as matters for this poem, begins to be discernible.

Anyone in the early 1730s who would level attacks that implicitly strike Walpole and even George II (339–42), who would praise Oxford, Bolingbroke, and Ormond (373–74), and who would refer to the later years of Queen Anne's reign as a "golden" dream (372) and to the Whigs as a "dangerous Faction" (379) would immediately be identified as a member of the Opposition. Swift supports this identification by giving the eulogist the loaded term *liberty*. The eulogist uses the word only once, but its importance is emphasized by the drumlike effect of its context:

"Fair LIBERTY was all his Cry;
"For her he stood prepar'd to die;
"For her he boldly stood alone;
"For her he oft expos'd his own.

(347–50)

The term, which earlier had been a Whig political slogan, came to be used in the late 1720s and the 1730s as the rallying cry for the anti-Walpole Opposition. The implications the word assumed for the Opposition may be illustrated from *The Craftsman*: "Let us act like wise Men; and remember that *Liberty* is the same divine Blessing, whether it be dispensed to us under a *Whig* or a *Tory* Administration; and that *arbitrary Power*, or any Degree of it, . . . receives some *Aggravation*, and becomes circumstantially *more grievous*, when it is introduced under the *Disguise*, and by the *pretended Champions* of *Liberty*."[39] Other details throughout the poem confirm the thematic importance of the contemporary political dispute. In the first half there is the inclusion of Swift's new friend Pulteney among his old friends Bolingbroke, Arbuthnot, Gay, and Pope (47–66). There is the high praise of that "excellent Paper, called the *Craftsman*," referred to twice, with another mention of Pulteney (194n, 274). And there are the cuts at "the Scriblers of the prevailing Party," who will libel Swift after his death (168n, 277n). The various references to contemporary politics simultaneously link the eulogist with the Opposition and attack the tyrannical ways of Walpole and the Whigs.

The conjunction of the eulogist's devotion to Opposition politics with an overly complimentary opinion of Swift suggests that the eulogy is not an objective recognition of Swift's merits and achievements, but an idealized portrait of Swift as the embodiment of the values the eulogist associates with the Opposition. It is a political speech, delivered to an already convinced audience, in a tavern whose disrepute should have been warning enough to regard the speaker with suspicion. Before his speech it could be said of the eulogist, as it was said earlier of other persons, "It is hardly understood, / Which way my Death can do [him] good" (77–78), but the eulogist too has "private Ends" (76). The eulogist becomes a further, concrete, dramatic example of the self-love and selfish interests exemplified throughout the first half of the poem, a final illustration of the truth of La Rochefoucauld's maxim, as he uses Swift's death as the occasion, not for an unselfish bestowal of the praise Swift's life deserves, but for a speech which invokes Swift's image in order to advance the eulogist's continuing campaign against the Whig party and the Walpole administration.

That this may indeed be the eulogist's role is supported by the final couplet: " 'That Kingdom he hath left his Debtor, / 'I wish it soon may have a Better." The lines seem uncomplimentary as a conclusion to a eulogy or an apologia, and a weak ending for the poem. Therefore, Pope and William King, in preparing the London edition of the poem in 1739, replaced them with the ending of "The Life and Genuine Character of Doctor Swift," partly, as King admits, "because I did not well understand them" (*Corres.*, V, 140). But if the speaker is less concerned with eulogizing Swift than with promoting his own political cause, he could be expected to hope that a successor to this Tory ideal will soon appear. And the self-centeredness of this final disregard of Swift provides a fine concluding note to the poem.

Swift in all likelihood was at least partially serious about the praise he put into the mouth of the eulogist in hyperbolized form. He desired recognition for his achievements, and he sought particularly the praise of respected friends. The other poems on himself show Swift seeking a method of perpetuating his memory through another's words, most notably in "The Life and Genuine Character," where a Tory speaker defends Swift straightforwardly against the libels of a Whig speaker. But Swift seems to have felt uncomfortable about such direct self-praise, even if delivered through a speaker's mouth, and sought, in the "Verses," a different vehicle—the "objective" explanatory notes and the ironic adulation of the eulogist. Swift was aware that he wanted to be remembered for who he was and what he had achieved, but when his friends have forgotten him within a month and his proud achievements are soon reduced to a set of dull footnotes, the irony of it all is unmistakable. The things the eulogist brings out are things Swift knew he actually was proud of, but when his only praise a year after his death comes as a panegyric by an unknown, powerless politician dreaming with some cronies in a contemptible tavern, the adulation would have to make him flinch. And such flinching would be perfectly in keeping with the spirit of La Rochefoucauld and of the entire libel-panegyric motif.

V

The words *panegyric* and *libel* are not mentioned in "An Epistle to a Lady" (1733), but they are, in fact, the unifying motif of the poem. When the lady asks the poet to "Sing [her] Praise in Strain sublime" (57), she is, of course, asking Swift to write panegyric about her. The request is refused, both because panegyric is not truthful and because such flattery is harmful to the giver and the recipient: "For your Sake, as well as mine, / I the lofty Stile decline" (217–18). Instead of panegyric, he writes raillery, "That Irony which turns to Praise."[40] First he puts claims for valid recognition into the lady's mouth:

> In Good Manners, am I faulty?
> Can you call me rude, or haughty?
> Did I e'er my Mite withold
> From the Impotent and Old?
> (69–72)

Since these claims are not disputed, they stand as indirect, but true praise of her, more desirable to Swift than the flights of panegyric. He goes on to backhanded praise, dismissing as unimportant the good values which really matter most:

> Tho' you lead a blameless Life,
> Are an humble, prudent Wife;
> Answer all domestick Ends,
> What is this to us your Friends?
> (99–102)

Even though the lady does admit to some faults (15–20), the first part of the poem, which apparently was written in the late 1720s, during one of Swift's visits to the home of Sir Arthur Acheson, stands as a witty, convincing tribute to Lady Acheson, a woman Swift much admired.

The "later addition," as Williams refers to the section beginning at line 133 (*Poems*, II, 629), is united with the earlier section by neither structure nor tone. Only when seen as the other half of the panegyric-libel theme do the two sections of the poem combine in any meaningful sort of whole. The latter half of the poem, despite its claims to the contrary, basically concerns libel. It has been called a Horatian apologia for Swift's satire;[41] it is not, by tone or content. To view it as Horatian and to cite it as an example of Swift's satiric theory is to give attention to only a few lines taken out of context.[42] Swift, it is true, does claim that "Ridicule has greater Pow'r / To reform the World, than Sour" (199–200) and that "From the Planet of my Birth, / I encounter Vice with Mirth" (141–42). But such assertions are rendered ironic by other lines in the poem:

> Let me, tho' the Smell be Noisom,
> Strip their Bums; let CALEB hoyse 'em;
> Then, apply ALECTO's Whip,
> Till they wriggle, howl, and skip.
> (177–80)

Later he asserts,

> As my Method of Reforming,
> Is by Laughing, not by Storming.
> (For my Friends have always thought
> Tenderness my greatest Fault.)
> (229–32)

If one could not verify the lack of tenderness from Swift's other works, this poem itself would supply proof enough that such a claim on Swift's part is ironic:

> You are not so great a Grievance
> As the Hirelings of *St. Stephan's.*
> You are of a lower Class
> Than my Friend Sir *Robert Brass.*
> None of these have Mercy found:
> I have laugh'd, and lash'd them round.
> (243–48; contractions expanded)

The irony itself is comic, of course, but the humor sets off and intensifies the attack. Although Swift claims that "Like the ever-laughing Sage, / In a Jest I spend my Rage" (167–68), he cannot, like Democritus, dismiss the evils of a ridiculous species, and he seems to find release for his rage only when his jests attack and expose the evils he sees: "Tho' it must be understood, / I would hang them if I could" (169–70). And although he claims that "All the Vices of a Court, / Do but serve to make me Sport" (147–48), Swift cannot, like Horace, be content to ridicule the follies and frailties of mankind. Again the context reveals the irony: "Shou'd a Monkey wear a Crown, / Must I tremble at his Frown?" (149–50). Swift counters vice, not with mirth, but with fierce attacks coated with comedy:

> Could I not, thro' all his Ermin,
> Spy the strutting chatt'ring Vermin?
> Safely write a smart Lampoon,
> To expose the brisk Baboon?
> (151–54)

This is not jest or ridicule, but libel, and Swift can hardly be un-aware of the irony of prefacing this passage with still another claim to objective detachment: "Wicked Ministers of State / I can easier scorn than hate" (143–44). The passages vilifying the king and prime minister make "scorn" ironic in both of its senses—"to deride" and "to disdain." The extent and depth of the evil he sees in the political scene (lines 173–80 bring the Opposition leaders into a central position) impel Swift past derision to libel, and past disdain to passion.

> Deuce is in you, Mr. DEAN;
> What can all this Passion mean?
> Mention Courts, you'll ne'er be quiet;
> On Corruptions running Riot.
> (181–84)

Swift may assert again and again, by references to "Merriment" (208) and "Laughing" (230), that his satiric method is Horatian, but each time the theory is undercut by the practice within the poem itself.

In light of the other poems considered in this chapter, Swift's purposes and methods in the poem become clear. The evil evident in the ministry and court, the "Machinations brewing, / To compleat the Publick Ruin" (189–90), drive a good man past ridicule to rage. The references to encountering "Vice with Mirth" do not lay out a theory of satire which Swift was endorsing; rather, they serve as a foil to the "libels" which such a situation makes inevitable. And the lady's request for flattery is a reminder of the ministry and monarch's similar desires: the panegyrics of the slaves pulling Walpole along (160) force an honest man to counter with invective. It is an apologia, then, not for a Horatian type of satire, or for Swift's satiric approach in general, but for the harsh methods to which Swift was forced in the political satires. And, as in the other apologias, it is fundamentally a defense of Swift less as a writer or satirist than as a person, as a man who relished "*Truth* and *Reason*" (272) and who, as he wrote, was acting sincerely upon his basic sense of "Wrong and Right" (270).

VI

The motifs traced in this chapter appear for the last time in "On Poetry: A Rapsody" (1733), celebrated by many as Swift's finest poem. Goldsmith calls it "one of the best versified poems in our language, and the most masterly production of its author." For Craik, it "stands side by side with Pope's *Epistle to Augustus*, and transcends the latter in its force of sweeping sarcasm."[43] Although much has been written about its "wonderfully sustained . . . irony" and the intensity of its satire,[44] its overall structure and themes have received little attention. The unity and purpose of the poem are best understood and appreciated when viewed through the traditions examined in this chapter.

The first section of the poem (lines 1–70) takes up the difficulty and frustrations of writing poetry. With a fairly close parallel to Horace's *Ars Poetica*, Swift satirizes the way all—especially the untalented—try to write poetry, despite their lack of encouragement or reward.

> *Brutes* find out where their Talents lie:
> A *Bear* will not attempt to fly:
> A founder'd *Horse* will oft debate,
> Before he tries a five-barr'd Gate:
> A *Dog* by Instinct turns aside,
> Who sees the Ditch too deep and wide.
> But *Man* we find the only Creature,
> Who, led by *Folly*, fights with *Nature*;
> Who, when *she* loudly cries, *Forbear*,
> With Obstinacy fixes there.
> (13–22)

The main direction of the poem, however, is indicated already by echoes of the Delany poems and passing political jabs: "*Court, City, Country* want you [as a Poet] not; / You cannot bribe, betray, or plot" (47–48).

The second section (lines 71–278) describes the three steps in a hack writer's development, presented as advice to a young poet. The first step is to publish a trial poem. The aspiring author must decide what kind of poetry he is best suited for—"Whether your Genius most inclines / To Satire, Praise, or hum'rous Lines" (81–82); next, "rising with *Aurora*'s Light, / The Muse invok'd, sit down to write" (85–86); then, convey the poem "by Penny-Post to *Lintot*" (107); and see in print, at last, "A Bastard of your own begetting" (116). If critics damn the anonymous poem at Will's next day, the poet should listen, heed the criticism, and mend his faults: "The trivial Turns, the borrow'd Wit, / The *Similes* that nothing fit" (151–52). Again, political references point the ultimate direction of the poem:

> On A's and B's your Malice vent,
> While Readers wonder whom you meant.
> A publick, or a private *Robber*;

> A *Statesman*, or a South-Sea *Jobber*.
> A *Prelate* who no God believes;
> A [Parliament], or Den of Thieves.
>
>   (159–64)

The allusions to Walpole and the simile in line 123 ("Be silent as a Politician") strengthen the associations between poor poetry and politics which were hinted at early in the poem. The second step in the young poet's development is to become a party scribbler: "From Party-Merit seek Support; / The vilest Verse thrives best at Court" (185–86). The advice cuts two ways, at the hiring of party scribblers and at the level of taste among court and government figures. In order to advance in his new position, the poet should write in praise of the monarch:

> With Prudence gath'ring up a Cluster
> Of all the Virtues you can muster:
> Which form'd into a Garland sweet,
> Lay humbly at your Monarch's Feet;
>
> . . . .
>
> Your Garland in the following Reign,
> Change but their Names will do again.
>
>   (221–32)

The satire again is carried beyond poetry to politics in the richly ironic lines "For *Law* and *Gospel* both determine / All Virtues lodge in royal Ermine" (227–28). And the third step for the young poet is to become a literary critic, a "puny Judge of Wit" (236), as authoritative and tyrannical as a prime minister:

> He gives Directions to the Town,
> To cry it up, or run it down.
> (Like *Courtiers*, when they send a Note,
> Instructing *Members* how to Vote.)
>
>   (269–72)

Step by step the political emphasis increases, as the hack writer becomes a more and more influential citizen of Grub Street.

The third section of the poem (lines 279–410) describes the

political state of Grub Street. Not only critics but poets as well behave like politicians: "In ev'ry Street a City-bard / Rules, like an Alderman his Ward" (285–86). The link with politics is strengthened still more as such authors are referred to as "Jobbers in the Poets Art" (312), thus confirming them as hack writers— ones "employed to do a job," according to the *OED*'s first defi- nition—and identifying them with the premier politician, the "South-Sea *Jobber*" of line 162. Further judgment is leveled against these poets because they are not only politicians but republicans: "They plot to turn in factious Zeal, / *Duncenia* to a Common-weal" (379–80). Indeed, in Grub Street, as in George's court and Walpole's ministry, all values and characteristics are reversed. In nature, "The Greater for the Smallest watch" (321), but in Grub Street, "The Brave are worried by the Base" (328); the descendants of Grub Street lack the patriotism natural to most races: "Their filial Piety forgot, / Deny their Country like a Scot" (359–60); and in Grub Street, the difficulty is not to gain renown for writing well, but "To purchase Fame by writing ill" (368). The lines which illustrate the Grub Street version of renown recall the diving episode in the second book of *The Dun- ciad*:

> For, tho' in Nature Depth and Height
> Are equally held infinite,
> In Poetry the Height we know;
> 'Tis only infinite below.
> For Instance: When you rashly think,
> No Rhymer can like *Welsted* sink.
> His Merits ballanc'd you shall find,
> [The Laureat] leaves him far behind.[45]
>
> (389–96)

Swift has steadily increased the ties of bad literature and corrupt politics until the characteristics of "the *low Sublime*" (370) impli- cate both poets and politicians: "From bad to worse, and worse they fall, / But, who can reach the Worst of all?" (387–88). The worst can be reached, says Swift, only through panegyric:

> O, what Indignity and Shame
> To prostitute the Muse's Name,
> By flatt'ring [Kings] whom Heaven design'd
> The Plagues and Scourges of Mankind.
>
> (405-8)

Panegyric corrupts both poet and politician, diverts them from the high callings that are theirs, and thus creates the ultimate debasement of art and government.

The final section of the poem (lines 411-80)[46] presents a "panegyric" on the king, the court, and the ministry. This will not, we are assured, be unwarranted praise, for no praise can be too high: "Your Panegyricks here provide, / You cannot err on Flatt'ry's Side" (469-70). As the poets laureate did so often, Swift praises George Augustus by establishing an analogy to Caesar Augustus;[47] he alludes specifically to a passage in the sixth book of the *Aeneid*, where Anchises provides Aeneas with a preview of the glorious heritage ahead for Rome. Swift's lines "Tho' Peace with Olive bind his Hands, / Confest the conqu'ring Hero stands" (419-20) are set against these lines by Virgil, foreseeing a great hero in the future for Rome: "Silvius Aeneas, pariter pietate vel armis / egregius" ["Silvius Aeneas, like thee peerless in piety or in arms"].[48] The biting irony arises from Swift's omission of Virgil's word "piety" and the mention of qualities George conspicuously lacked: he was neither a hero nor a conqueror, and the olive bound his hands mainly because of Walpole's policies of peace at any cost. Swift's "praise" continues:

> *Hydaspes, Indus,* and the *Ganges,*
> Dread from his Hand impending Changes.
> From him the *Tartar,* and *Chinese,*
> Short by the Knees intreat for Peace.
>
> (421-24)

Footnotes in the 1735 Faulkner edition direct the reader to these lines on Caesar:

> Super et Garamantas et Indos
proferet imperium.

[He shall spread his empire past Garamant and Indian.][49]

> Ius imperiumque Phraates
Caesaris accepit genibus minor.

[Phraates, on humbled knees, has accepted Caesar's imperial sway.][50]

The hyperbole has a certain appropriateness for Caesar, conqueror of the farthest reaches of his world, which only emphasizes
by ironic contrast its inappropriateness for George: not only has
he not conquered the farthest reaches of his world, but his name
would be utterly unknown in them. This encomium, along with
the "praise" of Walpole (441–64), continues the theme of panegyrics upon public officials; but the poem also carries the theme
a step further, to illustrate such flattery coming from a contemporary hack poet, in the lines on Frederick Louis, the Prince of
Wales:

> Our eldest Hope, divine *Iülus*,
> (Late, very late, O, may he rule us.)
> What early Manhood has he shown,
> Before his downy Beard was grown!
>   (429–32)

The analogy between Frederick and Ascanius has overshadowed
another allusion in the lines, to Laurence Eusden's *A Poem
Humbly Inscribed To His Royal Highness Prince Frederick, On His
Safe Arrival in Great Britain, And on His being Created Prince of
Wales*. When Swift refers to Frederick's "downy Beard," he al-
most surely was playing his phrase off against these lines by the
Poet Laureate:

> But when a Beard, o'er thy smooth Chin display'd,
> Silent proclaimed Thee Man with thicken'd Shade.[51]

Eusden exemplifies perfectly the hack poet whose career the
poem has charted, and these lines attest to the quality of litera-

ture produced by such poets. Two lines in the early part of Eusden's poem nicely highlight Swift's theme in "On Poetry":

> I may record the Wonders of thy Youth,
> But still the Panegyric breaths the Truth.[52]

It is just such an attitude that the poems surveyed in this chapter are protesting. Swift asserts in "On Poetry: A Rapsody"—as he did in "Directions for a Birth-day Song," the poems to Delany, "Verses on the Death of Dr. Swift," and "An Epistle to a Lady"— that panegyric invariably has questionable motives, that it deceives its readers, and that it is particularly harmful when used to endorse public figures and policies which the poet actually should be exposing and attacking in the name of truth. But in these poems Swift also presents a defense of himself, as one who was a friend and associate of the great but did not flatter them, who served his country (as Examiner, Drapier, and Irish Patriot) and was libelled for it, and who vigilantly and persistently attacked evil and corruption though it cost him the advancement he thought he deserved—as one who had indeed done "something distinguishable" for which his betters sought him.

VI

With a Prophet's Voice and Power
The Poems on Ireland

The previous chapters have shown the steadily expanding place of allusions in Swift's major poetry. In the early odes and satires, they supply support for ideas and models for structure, but they seem extraneous, useful but dispensable additions to what Swift really was attempting in the poems. With the personal poems and the poems about women, Swift began to weave allusions into the texture of his verse, to use them to limit and focus meaning. By the time he wrote the later political poems, he had gained full control of his poetic artistry and was using allusions to unify his works and add to their tone and themes. Despite these achievements, however, Swift was not often able to attain in poetry the intensity and power of his greatest works in prose. The most notable exception is his last important poem, his finest verse satire, "The Legion Club." In it, Swift's handling of allusion becomes totally effective, as the poem's structure, theme, and tone grow out of a combination of biblical and classical sources which give the poem the prophetic spirit he had sought long before in the odes and heroic verse. Though it appears late in Swift's life, at least two years after his previous significant poem, "The Legion Club" does not stand alone; it is the product of a series of less successful poems on Ireland, which are of interest here as earlier illustrations of the prophetic tone Swift adopted when he spoke as the Irish Patriot.

I

Perhaps it is not entirely fair to call Swift a prophet, in view of his own attitude toward that label. His attitude toward the traditional view of the prophet as one divinely inspired, one afforded visionary insights into the future, is made abundantly clear in the *Mechanical Operation of the Spirit*: "There are three general Ways of ejaculating the Soul, or transporting it beyond the Sphere of Matter. The first, is the immediate Act of God, and is called, *Prophecy* or *Inspiration*."[1] But the prophet was also, traditionally, a courageous denouncer of corruption, one who stood alone against the unrighteous. That characteristic the satirist often has in common with the prophet. When Swift seeks divine authority for his satiric attacks and therefore writes with the vehemence of the prophets of old, perhaps the term can be useful in characterizing his work and helpful for understanding the way his contemporaries viewed Swift and his Irish writings. Deane Swift, at least, saw him as a prophet; in his comments on the Drapier's Letters, he identifies Swift with the prophet Moses, instructing the children of Israel in the laws of God: "Think not because that evil day is past, that in the womb of time there cannot be any further projects to undermine your liberties. . . . Read therefore and imbibe the political principles of DR. SWIFT; engrave them on the tablet of your hearts; teach them unto your children's children."[2] Early in his career Swift sought "a prophet's voice and prophet's pow'r" in his writing ("To Mr. Congreve," 1); at the end of his career he is recognized for having achieved them.

The prophetic character of the Irish works leading up to "The Legion Club" can be illustrated briefly. It appears first in the prose tracts, as Swift alerts Ireland to the perils that surround it: "The Danger of our Ruin approaches nearer; And therefore the Kingdom requires *New* and *Fresh Warning*."[3] Swift openly derives the authority for his warnings from God, not by direct inspiration but from the written word, Scripture. Biblical references run throughout the Irish tracts. Swift includes passages from the Psalms and the Apocryphal book Ecclesiasticus as epigraphs on the title page of the fifth Drapier's letter; he compares the English king, trying to squeeze all that he can from the Irish, to Pharoah; he asks, like the Psalmist, "How long, O Lord, righteous and true"; he delivers a biblical admonition to William Wood regarding his effort to force unwanted coins on the Irish ("It must needs be that Offences come; but Wo unto him by whom the Offence cometh"); and he chastises the Irish in words derived from Scripture: "The Psalmist reckons it an Effect of God's Anger, when *he selleth his People for Nought, and taketh no Money for them.* That we have greatly offended *God* by the Wickedness of our Lives, is not to be disputed."[4] Swift's reliance on Scripture places him squarely in the prophetic tradition as William Kerrigan describes it: "Prophecy appears throughout history as a protection against wrongdoing and falsehood, a kind of invulnerable authority. It is most noticeable as a tone of voice, an attitude toward men derived from a necessarily hidden attitude toward God."[5] Though he abhors the idea of direct inspiration, Swift finds the Bible an alternative and acceptable source of divine revelation to give power and authority to his words.

There is also in the Irish tracts a tone and manner typical especially of the biblical prophets. Swift's vigorous denunciations, sometimes using biblical quotations for emphasis, often resemble those of the Old Testament prophets:

If I tell you there is a Precipice under you, and that if you go forwards you will certainly break your Necks: If I point to it before your Eyes, must I be at the Trouble of repeating it every Morning? . . . I fear there are some few *Vipers* among us, who, for Ten or Twenty Pounds Gain, would sell their Souls and their Country; although at last, it would end in their own Ruin as well as ours. Be not like *the deaf Adder, who refuses to hear the Voice of the Charmer, charm he never so wisely.*[6]

Other times the issues, such as liberty, are so clear that the prophetic exhortation is sufficiently forceful and eloquent without the support of Scripture:

Were not the People of *Ireland* born as *free* as those of *England?* How have they forfeited their Freedom? Is not their *Parliament* as fair a *Representative* of the *People,* as that of *England?* . . . Are they not Subjects of the same King? Does not the same *Sun* shine over them? And have they not the same *God* for their Protector? Am I a *Free-man* in *England,* and do I become a *Slave* in six Hours, by crossing the Channel?[7]

Always there is the vivid detail a prophet requires to reach his hearers' imaginations and emotions:

As to this country, there have been three terrible years dearth of corn, and every place strowed with beggars, but dearths are common in better climates, and our evils here lie much deeper. Imagine a nation the two-thirds of whose revenues are spent out of it, and who are not permitted to trade with the other third, and where the pride of the women will not suffer them to wear their own manufactures even where they excel what comes from abroad: This is the true state of Ireland in a very few words. These evils operate more every day, and the kingdom is absolutely undone.[8]

And frequently there are the prophet's usual expressions of frustration because his warnings and admonitions are not being heeded: "As I have been telling it often in print these ten years past."[9]

Swift told Pope that what he wrote in defense of the Irish was "owing to perfect rage and resentment,"[10] but very little of that fervor shows through in the essays: they are serious, rational, convincing, carefully controlled. Most of Swift's poems on Ireland, on the other hand, were used as a release for the emotions he kept under such firm restraint in the tracts. In such poems as

"Tom Mullinex and Dick" (1728), "Clad all in Brown" (1728), "Traulus" (1730), "On the Irish Bishops" (1732), and "Judas" (1732) he allows himself to express his venom and anger freely— there is little artistic merit to redeem them. On occasion, however, he takes a poem more seriously, and the prophetic motif carries over into the poetry as well.

The earliest such example is the paraphrase of "Horace. Book I. Ode XIV" (1724). Much of the poem follows closely the metaphor from Horace "*Betwixt a State, and Vessel under Sail*" (6).

> Unhappy Ship, thou art return'd in Vain:
> New Waves shall drive thee to the Deep again.
> Look to thy Self, and be no more the Sport
> Of giddy Winds, but make some friendly Port.
> Lost are thy Oars that us'd thy Course to guide,
> Like faithful Counsellors on either Side.
>   (9–14)

Horace's thought and expression are similar:

> O navis, referent in mare te novi
> fluctus. o quid agis! fortiter occupa
>   portum. nonne vides, ut
>   nudum remigio latus?

[Oh ship, new billows threaten to bear thee out to sea again. Beware! Haste valiantly to reach the haven! Seest thou not how thy bulwarks are bereft of oars?][11]

Swift's lines paraphrase Horace's closely and capture their tone of prophetic warning, low-keyed and thoughtful but full of emotion, as he endeavors to persuade the Romans not to suffer Augustus to abandon the government of the Empire.[12]

As Swift departs from his source, the prophetic tone becomes stronger, reminiscent of biblical prophecy and of the warning note in his early odes.

> Thy Mast, which like some aged Patriot stood
> The single Pillar for his Country's Good,

> To lead thee, as a Staff directs the Blind,
> Behold, it cracks by yon rough *Eastern* Wind.
>   (15–18)

The emotional parts of these lines are Swift's additions to Horace's simple statements of fact:

> Et malus celeri saucius Africo
> antemnaeque gemant.

[How thy shattered mast and yards are creaking in the driving gale.]

The emotional references to "aged Patriot" and "his Country's Good" prepare for the reference to blindness, a favorite technique of prophecy. One recalls Israel wandering "as blind men in the streets" (Lam. 4:14) and Christ's cry "Woe unto you, ye blind guides" (Matt. 23:16), as well as Swift's own lines on the "Blind and thoughtless Croud" in the "Ode to the Athenian Society" (87). The prophetic note enters again as Swift expands Horace's single line "non di, quos iterum pressa voces malo" ["nor hast thou gods to call upon when again beset by trouble"] to four lines which proclaim the central message of the poem:

> A larger Sacrifice in Vain you vow;
> There's not a Pow'r above will help you now:
> A Nation thus, who oft Heav'ns Call neglects,
> In Vain from injur'd Heav'n Relief expects.
>   (33–36)

The allusion to sacrifice recalls the Israelites' constant efforts to appease their God and to avert anticipated doom by sacrifice, and the repeated reply, "To do justice and judgment is more acceptable to the Lord than sacrifice."[13] Such calls to obedience are strengthened by warnings that the words of the prophet must not be disregarded.

And now, because ye have done all these works, saith the Lord, and I spake unto you, rising up early and speaking, but ye heard not; and I called you, but ye answered not; therefore . . . I will cast you out of my sight. . . . Pray not thou for this people, neither lift up cry nor prayer for them, neither make intercession to me: for I will not hear thee. (Jer. 7:13–16)

The Irish Patriot uses similar techniques:

If so wretched a State of Things would allow it, methinks I could have a malicious Pleasure, after all the Warning I have in vain given the Publick, at my own Peril, for several Years past. . . . *Wisdom crieth in the Streets; because I have called and ye refused; I have stretched out my Hand, and no Man regarded. But ye have set at nought all my Counsel, and would none. of my Reproof. I also will laugh at your Calamity, and mock when your Fear cometh.*[14]

The warning to pay heed, with dire predictions of the consequences of failure to do so, runs throughout Swift's essays on Ireland. But Irish hearts, like Israelite hearts, are "waxed gross, and their ears are dull of hearing, and their eyes they have closed" to the truth being proclaimed to them.[15]

The core of that truth comes out in a simile Swift adds to elaborate on Horace's line "nil pictis timidus navita puppibus / fidit" ["yet the timid sailor puts no faith in gaudy sterns"]. Swift's lines are

> In Ships decay'd no Mariner confides,
> Lur'd by the gilded Stern, and painted Sides.
> So, at a Ball, unthinking Fools delight
> In the gay Trappings of a Birth-Day Night:
> They on the Gold Brocades and Satins rav'd,
> And quite forgot their Country was enslav'd.
> (47–52)

The central proclamation of the poem is that of all Swift's words as Irish Patriot: "*Poor floating Isle . . . the Land of Slaves*" (1–2); "Thus, Commonwealths receive a foreign Yoke, / When the strong Cords of Union once are Broke" (21–22);[16] "Yet from an Empress, now a Captive grown, / She saved *Britannia*'s Right, and lost her own" (45–46). To this the Irish must listen and upon it they must act if there is to be any improvement in their situation: "The Remedy is wholly in your own Hands; and therefore I have digressed a little, in order to refresh and continue that *Spirit* so seasonably raised amongst you; and to let you see, that by the Laws of GOD, of NATURE, of NATIONS, and of your own Country, you ARE and OUGHT to be as FREE a People as your Brethren in *England*."[17]

The prophetic tone running through the paraphrase of Horace appears more briefly in other poems. In "Traulus. The first Part" (1730), a ringing defense of that tone expands the poem from a narrow, personal attack on Lord Allen to a broad denunciation of the corruptions and evil in Ireland which Lord Allen exemplifies so well:

> But *Ireland*'s Friends ne'er wanted Foes.
> A Patriot is a dang'rous Post
> When wanted by his Country most;
> Perversely comes in evil Times,
> Where Virtues are imputed Crimes,
> His Guilt is clear the Proofs are pregnant,
> A Traytor to the Vices regnant.
>   (88–94)

A biblical allusion in the following lines further broadens the meaning and stresses the prophetic aspect of the patriot's role:

> What Spirit since the World began,
> Could *always* bear to *Strive with Man*?
> Which God pronounc'd he never wou'd,
> And soon convinc'd them by a Floud.
> Yet still the D[ean] on Freedom raves,
> His Spirit always strives with Slaves.
> 'Tis Time at last to spare his Ink,
> And let them rot, or hang, or stink.
>   (95–102)

The context of the allusion from Genesis reinforces the sense of doom through which Swift has been warning Ireland: "And the Lord said, My spirit shall not always strive with man, for that he also is flesh: yet his days shall be an hundred and twenty years. . . . And God saw that the wickedness of man was great in the earth. . . . And the Lord said, I will destroy man whom I have created from the face of the earth; . . . for it repenteth me that I have made them" (Gen. 6:3–7). Much of the evil against which the Patriot declaims, and the source of Ireland's destruction, is external: the "Slavery and Destruction of a poor innocent Country" are inflicted by another people. "*Is it, was it, can it,* or *will it* ever be a Question . . . whether such a Kingdom should be *wholly undone, destroyed, sunk, depopulated,* made the Scene of *Misery* and *Desolation,* for the Sake of *William Wood?* God, of his infinite Mercy, avert this dreadful Judgement; and it is our universal *Wish,* that God would put it into *your* Hearts to be his Instruments for so good a Work."[18] But much of the selfishness and corruption against which Swift warns, much of the responsibility for the failure to avert Ireland's destruction, lies with the Irish themselves: "It is to gratify the vanity and pride, and luxury of the women, and of the young fops who admire them, that we owe this insupportable grievance of bringing in the instruments of our ruin."[19] Thus the Dean, in verse and prose, continues to rave on freedom and to strive with slaves, hoping to induce the spirit and wisdom needed to follow the remedies he regularly proposed to mitigate the poverty and suffering of the Irish.

Such a prophetic note is struck also in "On the Words—*Brother Protestants, and Fellow Christians,* so familiarly used by the Advocates for the Repeal of the *Test Act* in *Ireland, 1733.*" The tone and theme of the poem are indicated by the opening paragraph:

> An Inundation, says the Fable,
> O'erflow'd a Farmer's Barn and Stable;
> Whole Ricks of Hay and Stacks of Corn,
> Were down the sudden Current born;
> While Things of heterogeneous Kind,
> Together float with Tide and Wind;
> The generous Wheat forgot its Pride,
> And sail'd with Litter Side by Side;

> Uniting all, to shew their Amity,
> As in a general Calamity.
> A Ball of new-dropt Horse's Dung,
> Mingling with Apples in the Throng,
> Said to the Pippin, plump, and prim,
> *See, Brother, how we Apples swim.*
>   (1–14)

An allusion at the end, however, adds a more serious tone:

> While I, with humble *Job*, had rather,
> Say to Corruption—*Thou'rt my Father.*
> For he that has so little Wit,
> To nourish Vermin, may be *bit.*
>   (61–64)

The allusion to Job is mostly humorous. But a serious point lies behind it, again striking a note of warning and doom. With the allusion comes its context: "My days are past, my purposes are broken off, even the thoughts of my heart. . . . I have said to corruption, Thou art my father: to the worm, Thou art my mother, and my sister. And where is now my hope? as for my hope, who shall see it? They shall go down to the bars of the pit, when our rest together is in the dust" (Job 17:11–16). It is for Ireland as for the despondent, apparently dying Job; Swift too can see only darkness and inevitable failure, without any hope: "Therefore I repeat, let no Man talk to me of these and the like Expedients; till he hath, at least, a Glimpse of Hope, that there will ever be some hearty and sincere Attempt to put *them in Practice.*"[20] The time for proposing remedies calmly and reasonably is past; doom and destruction must be proclaimed, for they are imminent, and they may shock people into the drastic measures that are necessary.

II

The greatest of Swift's proclamations of destruction, damning the madness of the evildoers in Ireland, and his last major poem is "The Legion Club" (1736). Swift had been using the motifs of damnation and madness separately to attack the enemies of Ireland before he combined them in "The Legion Club." As far back as "Mad Mullinix and Timothy" (1728), a long invective against Richard Tighe, Swift had depicted Tim as even more insane than Mullinex. Mullinex asks Tim, "Why all this Clutter? / Why ever in these raging Fits?" (2–3); and the reason, which becomes evident as the poem proceeds, is that Tim is completely mad. Mullinex takes Tim under his wing and promises that within a week they will be indistinguishable: "Thus drest alike from Top to Toe, / That which is which, 'tis hard to know" (227–28). And in "Traulus, The first Part" (1730) Swift attacked Lord Allen by declaring him a son of the devil:

> Directing ev'ry Vice we find
> In Scripture, to the Dev'l assign'd:
> Sent from the Dark infernal Region
> In him they lodge, and make him *Legion.*
> Of *Brethren* he's *a false Accuser,*
> A Sland'rer, Traytor and Seducer;
> A fawning, base, trepaning Lyar,
> The Marks peculiar of his Sire.[21]
> (75–82)

But it was only as allusions enabled Swift to unite these two motifs that he could turn them into a poem deserving of the praise "The Legion Club" has received.[22] Borrowing from the *Aeneid* and the Bible, Swift brilliantly fused madness with damnation and the classical with the Christian to make "The Legion Club" his finest prophetic indictment in verse.

The poem's title and central metaphor—"These Demoniacs let me dub / With the Name of *Legion Club*" (11–12)—are biblical:

And when he was come out of the ship, immediately there met him out of the tombs a man with an unclean spirit. . . . He had been often bound with fetters and chains, and the chains had been plucked asunder by him, and the fetters broken in pieces: neither could any man tame him. . . . But when he saw Jesus afar off, he ran and worshipped him, and cried with a loud voice, and said, What have I to do with thee, Jesus, thou Son of the most high God? I adjure thee by God, that thou torment me not. For he said unto him, Come out of the man, thou unclean spirit. And he asked him, What is thy name? And he answered, saying, My name is Legion: for we are many. (Mark 5:2–9)

This passage supplies Swift with many of the terms which shape and direct the poem.[23] The biblical assumption that insanity is a result of demonic possession links madness with damnation in a highly suggestive way. A description of the behavior of a madman is provided, ready to be given further details and contemporary application. And the conflict of Christ against the devils serves as a justification for Swift's satire. Like Christ, he is right in going out to "torment" these devils whom no one else has been able to tame.

The opening seventy-four lines define the poem's governing metaphors of madness and damnation. The damnation motif is introduced in lines 5–8:

> By the prudent Architect
> Plac'd against the Church direct;
> Making good my Grandames Jest,
> *Near the Church*—you know the rest.

The double meaning of "against," implying spiritual remoteness as well as physical juxtaposition, and the proverb "Near the Church and far from God"[24] establish the Irish Parliament as a conscious opponent of God, an implication which arises from the immediate occasion of the poem, the struggle regarding the clergy's tithes. The issue, in Swift's eyes, involved the very survival of the church. The income of already poor Irish clergymen had declined as the movement from farming to grazing reduced the amount of tilled land, upon which regular tithes were assessed. So the clergy sought to collect the tithe of agistment, a levy on pasturage, which had a long but disputed existence. In March

1735/36, upon pressure from the graziers, the House of Commons passed a resolution declaring the tithe grievous and burdensome and urging resistance to it, particularly by forcing the clergy into court to collect it.[25] Lines 33-34 spell out the results of such opposition to God and reassert the motif of damnation: "And the Gospel will inform us, / He can punish Sins enormous."

The sense of evil pervading the opening section is extended by the allusion in line 28 to "the Den of Thieves." The source of the allusion, of course, is biblical: "And Jesus went into the temple of God, and cast out all them that sold and bought in the temple, and overthrew the tables of the money changers, and the seats of them that sold doves, and said unto them, It is written, My house shall be called the house of prayer; but ye have made it a den of thieves" (Matt. 21:12-13). This passage, too, invokes the image of divine cleansing as an implicit defense of the verbal scourging applied by the poem and reveals the actual reason for such an attack on the Irish Parliament. The need for cleansing in Jerusalem and in Dublin arises from the transformation of an institution from its proper legal and divine functions (and Parliament in the eighteenth century retained the last vestiges of the latter[26]) to a corrupt, materialistic, self-interested distortion of its true nature.[27] If Christ was justified in attacking those in the Temple who were profiting at the expense of the people's devotion, Swift is justified in excoriating members of Parliament who enrich themselves at the expense of a faithful clergy.

The remainder of the opening section, through sight and sound, metamorphoses Parliament into a madhouse.

> While they sit a picking Straws
> Let them rave of making Laws;
> While they never hold their Tongue,
> Let them dabble in their Dung.
> (49-52)

Since this is one of Swift's few poems in trochaics, the meter itself is an aberration from the norm and becomes a stylistic analogue to the theme of madness. The unusualness of the style is extended by the alternation between seven- and eight-syllable lines.[28] Although neither type of line appears in a consistent pattern, the seven-syllable lines appear most often in narrative portions, where the masculine rhymes make the descriptive comment terse and biting (see lines 49–52 above). The eight-syllable lines, with their comically reductive feminine rhymes, tend to appear where Swift depicts the club's madness subjectively, from within:

> At the Parsons, *Tom*, Halloo Boy,
> Worthy Offspring of a Shoeboy,
> Footman, Traytor, vile Seducer,
> Perjur'd Rebel, brib'd Accuser.
>   (67–70)

The unusual verse form may be part of an attempt to achieve a poetic equivalent of the Hogarthian sketches Swift wishes for near the end of the poem (219–30). His delineation of the club—with its dramatic and realistic, as well as comic and moral, traits—parallels Hogarth's satire, particularly as it makes individuals stand out from the satiric situation for special attention. And his handling of the verse may correspond to Hogarth's use of firm, flowing, simple designs to convey a sense of reason and well-being, and of shifting, swirling, intricate designs to convey havoc and unreason.[29] In "The Legion Club" the firm masculine lines create a framework of sanity, order, and salvation which opposes the lunacy, chaos, and destruction of the club as reflected in the precipitous pace of the feminine lines.

In line 29, "Quite destroy that Harpies Nest," Swift introduces a classical allusion among the previously Christian references, thus increasing the virulence of the attack on the club, but also anticipating the expansion of the poem's range of implication effected by its imitation of the *Aeneid* in lines 75–242. The motif of madness is extended into the second portion of the poem with an explanation of the factual basis for the allegation of insanity:

> When she [Clio] saw three hundred Brutes,
> All involv'd in wild Disputes;
> Roaring till their Lungs were spent,
> Privilege of Parliament.
> (113–16; contractions expanded)

The motif of damnation is expanded in the second part of the poem and is carried to its logical destination, Hell (lines 84, 86, 137, 142, 184). But its implications are extended and the moral precepts which underlie the condemnation of Parliament are universalized by having Clio take the poet on a tour of Hell corresponding to, and specifically alluding to, Aeneas's trip to the underworld in the sixth book of the *Aeneid*.

Swift's imitation of Virgil is purposefully selective. He ignores the offerings to Hecate (*Aeneid*, VI, 236–63) and begins the trip instead with the appeal to the Muse:

> All ye Gods, who rule the Soul
> *Styx*, through Hell whose Waters roll!
> Let me be allow'd to tell
> What I heard in yonder Hell.
> (83–86; cf. *Aeneid*, VI, 264–67)

Swift follows Virgil by proceeding to the mouth of Hell, which in the *Aeneid* is surrounded by allegorical figures the hero attempts to destroy ("The Legion Club," 87–102; *Aeneid*, VI, 273–94), for the specters of poverty, grief, and care could be expected to hover about the door of the Irish Parliament. But Swift isolates Briareus for special and more lengthy treatment because of the satiric potential in his hundred hands:

> In the Porch *Briareus* stands,
> Shews a Bribe in all his Hands:
> *Briareus* the Secretary,
> But we Mortals call him *Cary*.
> (103–6; cf. *Aeneid*, VI, 287)

More significant variation from the Virgilian model appears as Swift, by neglecting Virgil's second and third regions of the underworld—the region of waters, with the boatman Charon, and the gloomy region, or Erebus (*Aeneid*, VI, 295–547)—eliminates those parts which do not correspond to the Christian Hell. Instead, Swift moves directly from the mouth of Hell to the region of Tartarus, or torment. In so doing he subtly identifies the gates at the jaws of Hell (*Aeneid*, VI, 273) with the gates to Tartarus guarded by Tisiphone (*Aeneid*, VI, 552–56), who becomes the "Keeper" in "The Legion Club" (133). By reducing the four lower regions of classical Hades to the single region "rapidus flammis ambit torrentibus amnis" ["encircled with a rushing flood of torrent flames"] (*Aeneid*, VI, 550),[30] Swift fuses the classical Hades with the Christian Hell, thus uniting his disparate Christian and classical sources and universalizing the moral scope of the poem. The conjunction of Hell and Hades is further signaled by the poet's question, "Is that Hell-featur'd Brawler / . . . Satan?" (137–38), as the poet apparently expects to meet the Devil of Christianity at the conclusion of a journey through classical Hell.

The poet's tour of Hell, like Aeneas's, pauses at Tartarus, the meeting place of the club; in fact, it will end there, for the Parliament House has no Elysium. The motifs of madness and damnation continue as Swift describes the members of the club in lines 137–218. The damnation theme is sustained by the parallel with the *Aeneid*, VI, 580–624, while the details in the descriptions extend the madness theme. This section of the *Aeneid*, like the models for the earlier parts of the poem, furnishes Swift both a structural pattern and a moral context, as his six groups of "Heroes" incur guilt by their association with the corresponding six figures or groups in Virgil.

The first figures in Virgil's list are the Titan brood, who "fulmine deiecti fundo volvuntur in imo" ["having been hurled down by the thunderbolt, writhe in the lowest abyss"] (*Aeneid*, VI, 581). From the medieval commentators on Virgil, if not from Hesiod (*The-*

ogony, 147-210, 629-735), Swift would have known the two things generally stressed about the Titans: their ancestry, as unwanted children of Uranus,[31] and their rebellion against their father.[32] Swift, correspondingly, brings in the ancestor of his first hero, John Waller: "*Jack, the Grandson of Sir Hardress*" (140). Hardress Waller, a well-known leader of the Puritan rebellion, was a judge of Charles I, a signer of his death warrant, and a leader in Cromwell's reconquest of Ireland.[33] Invoking Sir Hardress not only establishes a link with the Titans, but also suggests that John Waller's vote against the clergy and his withholding of tithes from Roger Thorp (*Poems*, III, 835n) share the unholy nature of Cromwell's destructive campaign and of the rebellion and regicide in England: "In his Looks are Hell and Murther" (142).

Virgil mentions next the Aloean Twins, also thrown to Hell for their rebellion against the gods. Parallel to the twins are "the Puppy Pair of *Dicks*" (146), Richard Tighe and Richard Bettesworth, whose main rebellion has been against God's established church: "By their lanthorn Jaws and Leathern, / You might swear they both are Brethren" (147-48; see also *Poems*, III, 772-82 and 809-13). A further parallel suggests itself, although it derives from a legend not used by Virgil. At least one commentator mentions that, according to Hyginus, the Aloeids were bound to a column by serpents;[34] Swift thinks that the puppies may be tamed if they are tied "in a Tether" and lashed with "Scorpion Rods" (153, 158).

The correspondences between the next three groups are more oblique. John Wynne's torpidness (159-72) is ironically unlike the ambitious tyranny of Salmoneus,[35] although his pretense at being a legislator, awaking "Just to yawn, and give his Vote" (170), parallels Salmoneus, "flammas Iovis et sonitus imitatur Olympi" ["aping Jove's fires and the thunders of Olympus"] (*Aeneid*, VI, 586). The Allens, Jack and Bob (173-80), share with Tityus a questionable ancestry. While Tityus's parentage is uncertain ("By some Tityus was said to be a son of Terra, by others nourished by Terra"[36]), the Allens' is too well known:

> Son and Brother to a Queer,
> Brainsick Brute, they call a Peer.
> We must give them better Quarter,
> For their Ancestor trod Mortar.
>   (175-78)

And if Clements, Dilks, and Harrison—who have "Every Mischief in their Hearts" (187)—are like Ixion and Pirithous, they must be capable at least of ingratitude, attempted kidnapping, kidnapping, murder, and constant libidinousness.[37] Lest the reader take these heroes too seriously, however, Swift contrasts them with really great sinners. Of the Allens, the poet continues, "If they fail 'tis Want of Parts" (188); of Virgil's characters, on the other hand, Tisiphone says, "ausi omnes immane nefas ausoque potiti" ["all dared a monstrous sin, and what they dared attained"] (*Aeneid*, VI, 624).

Virgil climaxes his survey of Tartarus with a general denunciation of the most heinous crimes—sins of perversion and faithlessness. Swift uses this passage to set the context for his attack on Marcus Antonius Morgan, "Chairman to [the] damn'd Committee" (191) which considered the graziers' petition. If the previous three parallels to Virgil seem fairly incidental, Swift makes the final one essential, at least for a full understanding of several details in the attack. When Swift alludes to Morgan's university training, for example, he is creating the satiric equivalent to those whom Virgil condemns for having "invisi fratres, . . . pulsatusve parens" ["hated their brethren, or smote a sire"] (*Aeneid*, VI, 608-9):

> *Alma Mater* was thy Mother,
> Every young Divine thy Brother.
> Thou a disobedient Varlet,
> Treat thy Mother like a Harlot!
>   (199-202)

The personification of Morgan's books as injured women (especially in line 208) suggests that Morgan has been as unfaithful to his training and beliefs as those "ob adulterium caesi" ["slain for adultery"] were to their mates (*Aeneid*, VI, 612):

> When you walk among your Books,
> They reproach you with their Looks;
> Bind them fast, or from the Shelves
> They'll come down to right themselves.
> (207–10)

Morgan also, by betraying the clergy, shares the treachery of those who are in Tartarus for selling out their countries: "Vendidit hic auro patriam dominumque potentem / imposuit; fixit leges pretio atque refixit" ["This one sold his country for gold, and fastened on her a tyrant lord; he made and unmade laws for a bribe"] (*Aeneid*, VI, 621–22).

> Hast thou been so long at School,
> Now to turn a factious Tool!
> . . . .
> Thou, ungrateful to thy Teachers,
> Who are all grown reverend Preachers!
> . . . .
> While you in your Faction's Phrase
> Send the Clergy all to graze.
> (197–98, 203–4, 215–16)

One does not need the commentators to know that the man most famous in history and literature for bearing "arma . . . impia" (*Aeneid*, VI, 612–13) and for dying at least partly "ob adulterium" was the original bearer of Morgan's "heathenish Christian name" (*Corres.*, IV, 442). The parallel fits. Morgan, once a friend (*Corres.*, IV, 427, 434), now has turned his coat and been "Metamorphos'd to a Gorgan" (194). If accurate drawings do reveal "All the Soul in every Face" (230), Morgan's "horrid Looks" (195) are an external manifestation of his internal moral degradation. His endorsement of a corrupt and perfidious bill opposes his Christian and moral training as much as Mark Antony's actions were opposed to the virtues and values of Rome (*Aeneid*, VIII, 675–713).

Both Swift and Virgil despair of listing all the inhabitants of Hell: Virgil lacks "linguae centum . . . oraque centum, / ferrea vox" ["a hundred tongues, a hundred mouths, and voice of iron"] (*Aeneid*, VI, 625–26), which would not even be sufficient; and Swift reluctantly leaves "Half the best . . . behind" (236). But neither needs to name them all, for the specific examples illustrate a general theme. Running throughout Virgil's list is the thread of impiety. The commentators emphasize it for Salmoneus: "Virgil recognized this man as impious, and so have nearly all. For Didymus in Homer calls him 'impious'; Hesiod calls him 'unjust' and 'most arrogant.' Galenus, which I saw in Junius, 'evil hearted.' Suidas, following the same line, 'impious.' "[38] But they mention it for others as well. For the Titans: "On the first edge [of Tartarus] he puts together the heinous Titan clan, who he says because of singular impiety against the gods struggle in the depths of hell." For the Aloeids: "In truth since these young men were impious, they were punished for their boldness." And for Phlegyas: "Phlegyas, king of Thessaly, was impious."[39] The Tartarian passage begins with "ad impia Tartara" (543) and ends with "arma secuti / impia" (612–13). The greatest sin is opposed to the chief virtue of "pius Aeneas" (VI, 9, and elsewhere), as he builds his nation in obedience to the gods. Running through Swift's attack are both classical and Christian implications of impiety. In Swift's eyes the resolution passed by the House of Commons was a betrayal of patriotic duty as well as a sacrilege:

> Always firm in his Vocation,
> For the Court against the Nation.
> (171–72)

> But before the Priest he fleeces
> Tear the Bible all to Pieces.
> (65–66)

The action taken by the Commons and the actions it recommended to the graziers are completely opposite to those of Aeneas: they are disobedient to God and destructive to the nation.

For Swift to attack the members of the Irish Parliament, then, is as entirely justified as the cleansing of the Temple or the warning "iustitiam moniti et non temnere divos" ["learn ye to be just and not to slight the gods"] (*Aeneid*, VI, 620). From the Christian viewpoint, they—with all those who believe not and whose deeds are evil—are condemned already. Swift knew, as he wrote the last line, that the optative mood expresses action continuing in the present as well as action to begin in the future: "May their God, the Devil confound 'em" (242). And from the classical viewpoint as well, they deserve damnation for their sins against the gods and against their fellow men. Joseph Spence's comment on Tartarus sums up the appropriateness of using the *Aeneid* to attack the Irish Parliament:

In this horrid part, Virgil places two sorts of souls: first of such, as have shewn their impiety and rebellion toward the gods; and secondly of such, as have been vile or mischievous among men. Those . . . who were despisers of justice, and betrayers of their country; and who made and unmade laws, not for the good of the public, but only to get money to themselves. All these, and the despisers of the gods, Virgil places in this most horrid division of his subterraneous world; and in the vast abyss, which was the most terrible part even of that division.[40]

By his selective use of Virgil and the Bible, Swift gains authority for his venomous attack on men who were, in his eyes, guilty of both impiety and injustice. The dual sources provide a universal standard for the condemnation of corrupt legislators. Both Christian and classical worlds condemn such men, justify exposure of their deeds in harshest terms, and sentence them to the most terrible of punishments. With such far-reaching precedents as vindication, Swift in "The Legion Club" exposes, condemns, and punishes in one magnificent sweep of the pen.

Conclusion

In a letter to Charles Wogan, Swift called himself "only a Man of Rhimes, and that upon Trifles," but he went on to assert, "yet never any without a moral View."[1] The uses of allusion analyzed in this book resolve the paradox between trifling verse and morality. Swift, after his early odes, did not attempt the modes of poetry respected by his contemporaries as serious and dignified; but in the narrow area of verse to which he limited himself, he achieved, through his use of allusions, poems of value for their artistry and meaning. Through allusions he reinforced or expanded the meaning, structure, and tone of his verse and developed the truth he regarded as essential to it. And the improvement in his handling of those allusions, the growth of his reliance upon allusions and of his ability to integrate them with the rest of the poem, becomes an important measure of the advance in his technical skills as a poet. Allusions are, then, indispensable to our knowledge of Swift both as a man and as an artist.

No poem better illustrates this than "The Legion Club." Some critics have accused it of lacking control. Bonamy Dobrée calls it "scarcely controlled vituperation," and Oliver Ferguson refers to "the uncontrolled ferocity of his attack." As John Middleton Murry notes, however, "The emotion of the verses is violent, but the verse itself is perfectly controlled."[2] But Murry does not comment on the means by which such control was achieved. The poem's allusions enabled Swift to restrain and direct his feelings and his thoughts into what is surely "a diatribe almost unequaled in the literature of the world."[3] Such, to a lesser degree, is the case with all of Swift's major poems. Poetry for Swift could have remained the pleasant pastime it became after he abandoned the Pindarics, a light break from his serious efforts in prose—verse written with his "left Hand, [while he] was in great Haste, and the other Hand was employed at the same Time in writing some Letters of Business" (*Poems*, III, 968). As he discovered, particularly through experimenting with imitations, the effects he could achieve with allusions—the control of structure, the nuances of tone, and the added levels and shades of meaning—his poetry developed the range and power of his finest pieces.

And it is in allusions that the personal element appears most effectively in his poems. The desire for respect and affirmation that Swift experienced throughout his life, possibly because of the unsettled state of his childhood and youth, and surely because of his lack of "a blue riband, or of a coach and six horses" later (*Corres.*, III, 331), appears in the poems as well as in his letters and prose. Already in the odes Swift had discovered the value of placing himself at one with an honored tradition in order to justify what he was doing. When he moved into public life and had increased occasion for such defense, the strategy of alluding to and thus associating himself with respected writers emerges regularly. There is the use of Horace in the imitations, of Ovid in "Cadenus and Vanessa" and the scatological poems, of Opposition writers in the later political poems, and of Virgil in "The Legion Club." Self-vindication was a vital element

throughout Swift's poetry, and allusions provided him a vehicle
for endorsing himself strongly and yet subtly.

Swift's imitation of part of the First Satire of the Second Book
of Horace ("A Dialogue between an eminent Lawyer and Dr.
Swift" [1730]) nicely sums up the emphases of this study. Swift
inquired, as had Horace before him,

> What's your advice? shall I give o're,
> Nor ever fools or knaves expose
> Either in verse or hum'rous prose?
> (8–10)

The lawyer he has consulted, after advising Swift to "Forbear
your poetry and jokes, / And live like other christian fokes"
(17–18), picks out three significant qualities of Swift's work. He
emphasizes the importance of allusions: "And such as know
what *Greece* has writ / Must taste your irony and wit" (51–52);
he stresses the importance of truth: "Some by philosophers mis-
led, / Must honour you alive and dead" (49–50); and he admits
to Swift's effectiveness as a prophetic voice: "While most that
are or would be great, / Must dread your pen, your person hate"
(53–54). The aspects of his works stressed in this study, then, are
those Swift pointed out as the ones which led him to his fate:
"And you on DRAPIER's *Hill* must lye, / And there without a
mitre dye" (55–56). And appearing in "an allusion to the first
Satire of the second book of Horace," they reemphasize how absolutely essential attention to allusions is for a full understanding
and appreciation of Swift's verse.

Notes

Index

Notes

Abbreviations

Poems   *The Poems of Jonathan Swift*, ed. Harold Williams, 2nd ed., 3 vols. (Oxford: Clarendon Press, 1958). All quotations of Swift's poetry are from this edition and are cited by line numbers within parentheses in the text.

Prose Works   *The Prose Works of Jonathan Swift*, ed. Herbert Davis et al., 14 vols. (Oxford: Basil Blackwell, 1939–68).

Corres.   *The Correspondence of Jonathan Swift*, ed. Harold Williams, 5 vols. (Oxford: Clarendon Press, 1963–65).

Introduction

1   9 September 1730, *Corres.*, III, 407; contractions expanded.

2   "Horace, Lib. 2. Sat. 6" (1714), *Poems*, I, 199.

3   "To Stella, Who Collected and Transcribed his Poems" (1720), *Poems*, II, 729. For other discussions of the line, see Christine Rees, "Gay, Swift, and the Nymphs of Drury-Lane," *Essays in Criticism*, 23 (1973), 1–21, and Alan S. Fisher, "Swift's Verse Portraits: A Study of His Originality as an Augustan Satirist," *Studies in English Literature*, 14 (1974), 343–56.

4 Earl R. Wasserman, "The Limits of Allusion in *The Rape of the Lock*," *Journal of English and Germanic Philology*, 65 (1966), 443.

5 Earl R. Wasserman, *Pope's "Epistle to Bathurst": A Critical Reading with an Edition of the Manuscripts* (Baltimore: The Johns Hopkins Press, 1960), p. 11.

6 F. Elrington Ball, *Swift's Verse: An Essay* (London: John Murray, 1929), p. viii. For a recent exchange on Swift's use of personae or disguises in his prose, see Robert C. Elliott, "Swift's 'I,' " *Yale Review*, 62 (1973), 372–91, and Donald T. Siebert, Jr., "Masks and Masquerades: The Animus of Swift's Satire," *South Atlantic Quarterly*, 74 (1975), 435–45. The case against the persona was stated first by Irvin Ehrenpreis, "Personae," in *Restoration and Eighteenth-Century Literature: Essays in Honor of Alan Dugald McKillop*, ed. Carroll Camden (Chicago: University of Chicago Press, 1963), pp. 25–37. The best defense of the persona as a method in Swift is by James R. Wilson, "Encountering Vice with Mirth," in *His Firm Estate: Essays in Honor of Franklin James Eikenberry*, ed. Donald E. Hayden, The University of Tulsa Department of English Monograph Series, No. 2 (Tulsa, Okla.: The University of Tulsa, 1967), pp. 24–35.

7 Maurice Johnson, "Swift's Poetry Reconsidered," in *English Writers of the Eighteenth Century*, ed. John H. Middendorf (New York: Columbia University Press, 1971), pp. 239, 240.

8 Aubrey Williams, "Swift and the Poetry of Allusion: 'The Journal,' " in *Literary Theory and Structure: Essays in Honor of William K. Wimsatt*, ed. Frank Brady, John Palmer, and Martin Price (New Haven: Yale University Press, 1973), p. 242. Williams must be using *subtly* to mean "skillfully or cleverly; deftly" rather than "mysteriously, abstrusely," for his essay explicates Swift's use of an allusion which Swift mentions directly in the poem.

Chapter I: Cowley unto Himself

1 Norman Maclean, "From Action to Image: Theories of the Lyric in the Eighteenth Century," in *Critics and Criticism, Ancient and Modern*, ed. R. S. Crane (Chicago: University of Chicago Press, 1952), p. 408.

2 Swift to Thomas Swift, 3 May 1692, *Corres.*, I, 10, 9.

3 Irvin Ehrenpreis, *Swift—The Man, His Works, and the Age*, Vol. I: *Mr Swift and His Contemporaries* (London: Methuen, 1962), pp. 115–16, 130.

4 "Ode to the Athenian Society" (1692), l. 173.

5 See also "Ode to the King" (1690/91), ll. 13–18; "Ode to the Athenian Society," ll. 222–27, 277–82; "Ode to Sir William Temple" (1692), ll. 104–14, 191–95; and "Ode to Sancroft," ll. 27–40, 67–72, 162–65, 192–97, and 218–22.

6 The quotations in this sentence are from "Ode to the King," ll. 112–13; "Ode to the Athenian Society," ll. 127, 271; and "Ode to Sancroft," ll. 23, 40, 140–42.

7 From "Ode to the Athenian Society," l. 189; "Ode to the King," ll. 87–89; "Ode to Sancroft," ll. 101–6; and "Ode to the Athenian Society," ll. 1–7, respectively.

8 "Ode to the King," ll. 19–20; see also l. 33, and "Ode to Sancroft," ll. 7, 47, 143.

9 Williams, *Poems*, I, xlvi.

10 In his preface to the section *Pindarique Odes, Written in Imitation of the Stile & Manner of the Odes of Pindar*, in *The Works of Mr Abraham Cowley* (London, 1668), sig. T2^v. Subsequent comments on the ode by Cowley are from his preface to the volume as a whole, sig. C2^v. All quotations of Cowley's poems are from this edition.

11 Jean Loiseau, *Abraham Cowley's Reputation in England* (Paris: Henri Didier, 1931), p. 3.

12 *A Tale of a Tub, To which is added The Battle of the Books and the Mechanical Operation of the Spirit*, ed. A. C. Guthkelch and D. Nichol Smith, 2nd ed. (Oxford: Clarendon Press, 1958), p. 250.

13 Swift to Thomas Swift, 3 May 1692, *Corres.*, I, 8.

14 Swift to Jane Waring, 29 April 1696, *Corres.*, I, 21.

15 Robert Shafer, *The English Ode to 1660* (Princeton: Princeton University Press, 1918), p. 25.

16 R. C. Jebb, *The Growth and Influence of Classical Greek Poetry* (London, 1893), p. 161.

17 Shafer, *The English Ode to 1660*, p. 154. Carol Maddison, *Apollo and the Nine: A History of the Ode* (London: Routledge and Kegan Paul, 1960), pp. 371–73.

18 The latter quotation is from Thomas Sprat's "Account of the Life and Writings of Mr Abraham Cowley," prefaced to the 1668 edi-

tion of Cowley's *Works*, sig. b2ᵛ, as are subsequent comments by Sprat on the ode.

19 "Preface" to *Sylvæ* (1685; rpt. London: Scolar Press, 1973), sig. a7ᵛ. Reprinted in *Of Dramatic Poesy and Other Critical Essays*, ed. George Watson (London: J. M. Dent and Sons, 1962), II, 32.

20 James D. Garrison, *Dryden and the Tradition of Panegyric* (Berkeley and Los Angeles: University of California Press, 1975), shows how the conventions of panegyric, traditional since classical times, lose their meaning after Dryden: see especially pp. 243–57.

21 For discussions of the use of common forms to give structure and order to Swift's prose works, see the following: Miriam K. Starkman, *Swift's Satire on Learning in "A Tale of a Tub"* (Princeton: Princeton University Press, 1950), pp. 106–46, on the parody of Dryden's works in the *Tale*; Ricardo Quintana, *The Mind and Art of Jonathan Swift* (London: Oxford University Press, 1936), pp. 296–300, on the adaptation of the traditional imaginary voyage in *Gulliver's Travels*; and Charles A. Beaumont, *Swift's Classical Rhetoric*, University of Georgia Monographs, No. 8 (Athens: University of Georgia Press, 1961), pp. 15–43, on "A Modest Proposal" as classical oration. Other uses of common forms include the historical essay in *The Battle of the Books* and the ordinary religious tract in "An Argument against Abolishing Christianity." See also James I. Calderwood, "Structural Parody in Swift's *Fragment*," *Modern Language Quarterly*, 23 (1962), 243–53.

22 Ehrenpreis, *Swift*, I, 113, 118, and 129, notes a number of verbal allusions to Cowley. Other echoes of Cowley include "Ode to the King," l. 48 (cf. "The Thraldome," l. 7 and "34th Chapter of the Prophet Isaiah," l. 66), "Ode to Sir William Temple," ll. 87–88 (cf. "The Extasie," ll. 23–24), "Ode to Sir William Temple," ll. 62–64 (cf. "Ode. Upon occasion of a Copy of Verses of my Lord Broghills," ll. 77–82), and "Ode to Sir William Temple," ll. 180–81 (cf. "To the Lord Falkland," ll. 29–30).

23 "The Hind and the Panther" (1687), Part I, line 1, *The Poems of John Dryden*, ed. James Kinsley (Oxford: Clarendon Press, 1958), II, 470. Cf. "About [Io's] Milk-white neck, his arms he threw": "The first Book of Ovid's Metamorphoses" (1693), l. 901, *The Poems of John Dryden*, II, 823.

24 "A Letter to a Young Gentleman, Lately entered into Holy Orders" (1720), *Prose Works*, IX, 70.

25 Jer. 11:17; also 19:15, 34:5, 35:17, 36:7, and 40:2.

26 In a detailed study of the background and meaning, Edward W. Rosenheim, Jr., argues that the poem is complete as we have it; see "Swift's *Ode to Sancroft*: Another Look," *Modern Philology*, 73, No. 4, Part 2 (1976), S24–S39.

27 Kathryn Montgomery Harris, " 'Occasions so Few': Satire as a Strategy of Praise in Swift's Early Odes," *Modern Language Quarterly*, 31 (1970), 36.

28 Examples of satire in Swift's odes are lines 82–89 in the ode to the King; lines 81–85, 123–31, 180–85, 203–10, and 220–27 in the ode to the Athenian Society; and lines 92–103 in the ode to Temple. Cowley incorporates satire in the second stanza of "The Extasie," and Dryden in "Threnodia Augustalis" and the fourth stanza of the ode to Anne Killigrew.

29 E.g., "To the Right Honourable John Lord Sommers," *A Tale of a Tub*, pp. 22–27; "To Mrs. Biddy Floyd" (1708), *Poems*, I, 118; "On Stella's Birth-day" (1718/19), *Poems*, II, 721–22; "Stella's Birth-day" (1720/21), *Poems*, II, 734–36.

30 "I have seen fewer good panegyrics than any other sort of writing, especially in verse" (Swift to Thomas Beach, 12 April 1735, *Corres.*, IV, 320).

31 A valuable reading of "Occasioned by Sir W—— T——'s Late Illness and Recovery" is included in Robert W. Uphaus, "From Panegyric to Satire: Swift's Early Odes and *A Tale of a Tub*," *Texas Studies in Literature and Language*, 13 (1971), 55–70.

Chapter II: Needy Poet Seeking for Aid

1 Harold Williams (*Poems*, I, 78) follows Faulkner in dating the revision 1708. In text citations for these poems, "A" will designate the manuscript version and "B" the published version.

2 The best analysis of influences on Swift's poetry is by William K. Wimsatt, "Rhetoric and Poems: The Example of Swift," in *The Author in His Work: Essays on a Problem in Criticism*, ed. Louis L. Martz and Aubrey Williams (New Haven: Yale University Press, 1978), pp. 229–44.

3 "The History of Vanbrug's House" (1706), ll. 37–38, *Poems*, I, 87.

4 *Journal to Stella*, ed. Harold Williams (Oxford: Clarendon Press, 1948), I, 27.

5 Alan S. Fisher, commenting on the poem in "Swift's Verse Portraits: A Study of His Originality as an Augustan Satirist" (*Studies in English Literature*, 14 [1974], 346), relates the poem to Amphion rather than Orpheus. Either or both may have influenced Swift. I regard Orpheus as the more important because of William King's recent imitation of the story.

6 *Hercules Oetaeus*, 1036–44, *Seneca's Tragedies*, trans. Frank J. Miller, Loeb Classical Library (London: Heinemann, 1917), II, 271. Similarly, *The Merchant of Venice*, V, i, 79–80: "Therefore the poet / Did feign that Orpheus drew trees, stones, and floods" (*The Riverside Shakespeare*, ed. G. Blakemore Evans [Boston: Houghton Mifflin, 1974], p. 280).

7 Ovid, *Metamorphoses*, XI, 1–2, trans. Frank J. Miller, Loeb Classical Library (London: Heinemann, 1916), II, 121. Similarly, *Iphigenia at Aulis*, 1211–12, *Euripides*, trans. Arthur S. Way, Loeb Classical Library (London: Heinemann, 1912), I, 113.

8 "Orpheus and Euridice" (1704), ll. 21–22, *Miscellanies in Prose and Verse by William King* (London, [1709]), p. 370.

9 *A Tale of a Tub, To which is added The Battle of the Books and the Mechanical Operation of the Spirit*, ed. A. C. Guthkelch and D. Nichol Smith, 2nd ed. (Oxford: Clarendon Press, 1958), p. 231. All quotations from the *Tale* and *The Battle of the Books* are from this edition; page numbers for subsequent citations are given in the text. In this and several later quotations from the *Tale* and the *Battle*, I have silently changed italic type to roman to conform with modern editorial practice.

10 Unless otherwise noted, references to Pliny are from the *Natural History*, X, lxxxvi, 188, Vol. III of the Loeb Classical Library edition, trans. H. Rackham (London: Heinemann, 1940), p. 413.

11 *Natural History*, XXIX, xxiii, 76, Vol. VIII of the Loeb Classical Library edition, trans. W. H. S. Jones (London: Heinemann, 1963), p. 233.

12 On the invective technique in "The Description of a Salamander," see Robert W. Uphaus, "Swift's Poetry: The Making of Meaning," *Eighteenth-Century Studies*, 5 (1972), 572–74.

13 Douglas Bush, *Mythology and the Renaissance Tradition in English Poetry* (Minneapolis: University of Minnesota Press, 1932), p. 287.

14 Williams concludes that "this [date] may be accepted" (*Poems*, I,

89); but Irvin Ehrenpreis, *Swift—The Man, His Works, and the Age*, Vol. II: *Dr Swift* (London: Methuen, 1967), pp. 247–48n, places it "between the summer of 1707 and the autumn of 1708."

15 "Baucis and Philemon, Out of the Eighth Book of Ovid's Metamorphoses" (1700), *The Poems of John Dryden*, ed. James Kinsley (Oxford: Clarendon Press, 1958), IV, 1565–70.

16 It should be noted, however, that Williams (*Poems*, I, 89) and Ehrenpreis (*Swift*, II, 245n) agree that the "&c" at the end of the manuscript version of Swift's poem is meant to indicate that the poem is to go on substantially as it does in the printed version.

17 *Some Remarks on the Tale of a Tub. To which are Annexed "Mully of Mountown," and "Orpheus and Euridice"* (London, 1704), p. 33. Page numbers for subsequent citations are given in the text.

18 See Colin J. Horne, " 'From a Fable form a Truth': A Consideration of the Fable in Swift's Poetry," in *Studies in the Eighteenth Century*, ed. R. F. Brissenden (Canberra: Australian National University Press, 1968), pp. 196–98.

19 David Novarr, "Swift's Relation with Dryden, and Gulliver's *Annus Mirabilis*," *English Studies*, 47 (1966), 346. Also see Martin Price, *Swift's Rhetorical Art* (New Haven: Yale University Press, 1953), pp. 45–47.

20 Herbert Davis, "Swift's View of Poetry," in *Studies in English by Members of University College, Toronto*, collected by Malcolm W. Wallace (Toronto: University of Toronto Press, 1931), p. 31.

21 Eric Rothstein, "Jonathan Swift as Jupiter: 'Baucis and Philemon,' " in *The Augustan Milieu: Essays Presented to Louis A. Landa*, ed. Henry Knight Miller, Eric Rothstein, and G. S. Rousseau (Oxford: Clarendon Press, 1970), p. 213.

22 Roger Savage, "Swift's Fallen City: *A Description of the Morning*," in *The World of Jonathan Swift: Essays for the Tercentenary*, ed. Brian Vickers (Cambridge, Mass.: Harvard University Press, 1968), p. 177. But cf. William Ross Clark, "Poems for Teaching: 'A Description of the Morning,' " *Clearing House*, 35 (1961), 381–82, with David M. Vieth, "*Fiat Lux*: Logos versus Chaos in Swift's 'A Description of the Morning,' " *Papers on Language and Literature*, 8 (1972), 302–7.

23 Williams, *Poems*, I, 60. Similarly, F. Elrington Ball, *Swift's Verse: An Essay* (London: John Murray, 1929), p. 42.

24 William Walsh, *Letters and Poems, Amorous and Gallant* (London, 1692), p. 74.

25 Ehrenpreis, *Swift*, II, 385n.

26 Dryden's translations are quoted from Kinsley's edition of the *Poems*, Vols. II and III.

27 Brendan O Hehir, in a well-known essay on the poem, concludes that it is "an oblique denunciation of cathartic doom upon the corruption of the city" ("Meaning of Swift's 'Description of a City Shower,' " *ELH*, 27 [1960], 206). The results of O Hehir's unquestionably brilliant scholarship are overly ingenious, incompatible with the course of Swift's development as a poet, and inconsistent with the tone of the poem. Although Irvin Ehrenpreis does not mention O Hehir's essay in his "Meaning: Implicit and Explicit" (*New Approaches to Eighteenth-Century Literature*, ed. Phillip Harth [New York: Columbia University Press, 1974], pp. 117–55), it would exemplify the critical approaches he is criticizing for overattention to secondary elements of Augustan poems and failure to square expositions of an author's meaning with his explicit statements in the poems. John I. Fischer, "Apparent Contraries: A Reading of Swift's 'A Description of a City Shower,' " *Tennessee Studies in Literature*, 19 (1974), 21–34, in quite a different reading—that the poem is purposively ambivalent in order to teach us the limits of our capabilities—also goes well beyond "what the author might have expected his reader to get, [or] what the reader might reasonably attribute to the author" (Ehrenpreis, "Meaning," p. 155).

28 Ehrenpreis, *Swift*, II, 385n.

Chapter III: Thoughts Borrowed from Virgil and Horace

1 Texts and translations are from *Horace: Satires, Epistles, and Ars Poetica*, trans. H. Rushton Fairclough, Loeb Classical Library (London: Heinemann, 1926).

2 Philip Francis, *A Poetical Translation of the Works of Horace, With the Original Text, and Critical Notes collected from his best Latin and French Commentators*, 3rd ed. (London, 1749), II, 287n (hereafter cited as Francis). Similarly, André Dacier, *Les Oeuvres D'Horace, Tradvites en Francois, avec des Notes, et des Remarques Critiques sur tout L'ouvrage*, 2nd ed. (Paris, 1691), XIII, 262. The view accepted, for example, by Sanadon that the birthday being celebrated is that

of Caius Caesar, oldest son of Agrippa and Julia and heir apparent to the throne of Augustus, would make this poem all the more appropriate for imitation by Swift at a time when the royal succession in England was a matter of great concern (R. P. Sanadon, *Les Poésies D'Horace* [Paris, 1728], II, 424).

3 12 Charles II, 30, quoted by E. W. Rosenheim, Jr., "Swift and the Martyred Monarch," *Philological Quarterly*, 54 (1975), 179.

4 *The Harleian Miscellany*, VI (London, 1810), 599–600.

5 "*Archaici lecti* ce sont de vieux licts, des licts a la vieille mode, qui se sentoient de la modestie des premiers Romains, & qui n'estoient enrichis ni d'or ni d'yvoire, comme ceux que le luxe avoit fait inventer depuis quelque temps" (Dacier, VIII, 252). The manuscript reading, "Archiacis lectis," is accepted by Bentley and Sanadon. "Both the Scholiasts tell us, that Archias was a Person, who made Beds of a lower, shorter Kind" (Francis, II, 286n).

6 Keith Feiling, *A History of the Tory Party, 1690–1714* (Oxford: Clarendon Press, 1924), p. 409.

7 Sanadon, II, 422, trans. Francis (II, 286n).

8 *The Examiner*, No. 39, 3 May 1711, *Prose Works*, III, 142. Also, *The Examiner*, No. 35, 5 April 1711, *Prose Works*, III, 123.

9 [Abel Boyer], *The History Of the Reign of Queen Anne, Digested into Annals*, XI (London, 1713), 130.

10 A. Boyer, *The History of Queen Anne* (London, 1735), p. 578.

11 *Journal to Stella*, ed. Harold Williams (Oxford: Clarendon Press, 1948), II, 430.

12 *The History of the Four Last Years of the Queen* (1713), *Prose Works*, VII, 21.

13 Dacier, II, 10; Sanadon, I, 218.

14 *The Odes, Satyrs, and Epistles of Horace*, trans. Thomas Creech (London, 1684), p. 52.

15 The text and translation of the ode are from *Horace: The Odes and Epodes*, trans. C. E. Bennett, Loeb Classical Library (London: Heinemann, 1914).

16 "The Publick Spirit of the Whigs" (1714), *Prose Works*, VIII, 56.

17 Sanadon, I, 227, trans. Francis (I, 133n); also, Dacier, II, 39–40.

18 Sanadon, II, 361, trans. Francis (II, 304n). Dacier adds: "C'etoit un des plus grands Orateurs de son temps, & de plus, homme de grande qualité, & de très-grande consideration" (VIII, 385).

19 Swift to the Earl of Oxford, 19 July 1715, *Corres.*, II, 182.
20 Swift to Lord Halifax, 13 June 1709, *Corres.*, I, 142.
21 Irvin Ehrenpreis, *Swift—The Man, His Works, and the Age*, Vol. II: *Dr Swift* (London: Methuen, 1967), p. 743.
22 John M. Aden, *Something Like Horace: Studies in the Art and Allusion of Pope's Horatian Satires* (Nashville, Tenn.: Vanderbilt University Press, 1969), p. 102.
23 The lines are ascribed to Pope by William Warburton, *The Works of Alexander Pope* (London, 1751), VI, 19n; Joseph Warton, *The Works of Alexander Pope* (London, 1797), VI, 3; and Gilbert Wakefield, *The Works of Alexander Pope*, ed. William Lisle Bowles (London, 1806), VI, 14n. Cf. Williams, *Poems*, I, 197, and Ehrenpreis, *Swift*, II, 742n.
24 Ehrenpreis, *Swift*, II, 742n, attributes them to Pope, as do Reginald H. Griffith, *Alexander Pope: A Bibliography*, Vol. I, Part 2 (Austin: University of Texas Press, 1927), 378, and W. J. Courthope, in the Elwin-Courthope edition of *The Works of Alexander Pope*, III (London, 1881), 406n. Williams gives the lines to Swift (*Poems*, I, 197–98), while John Butt leaves the question open: "All of [this] is too ambiguous for certain ascription" (*Imitations of Horace*, ed. John Butt, Vol. IV of the Twickenham Edition of the Poems of Alexander Pope, 2nd ed., rpt. with corrections [London: Methuen, 1961], p. 248).
25 Reuben A. Brower, *Alexander Pope: The Poetry of Allusion* (1959; rpt. London: Oxford University Press, 1968), p. 173.
26 *Imitations of Horace*, p. 249.
27 Brower, *The Poetry of Allusion*, p. 284.
28 Studies of "Cadenus and Vanessa" have all too often been heavily influenced by use of external sources and have not treated it on its own terms as a poem. This is particularly true of the essays by Peter Ohlin (" 'Cadenus and Vanessa': Reason and Passion," *Studies in English Literature*, 4 [1964], 485–96) and James L. Tyne, S. J. ("Vanessa and the Houyhnhnms: A Reading of 'Cadenus and Vanessa,' " *Studies in Engish Literature*, 11 [1971], 517–34). Gareth Jones, in "Swift's *Cadenus and Vanessa*: A Question of 'Positives,' " *Essays in Criticism*, 20 (1970), 438, argues properly that "the response, in Swift's best verse, is built up by the complex totality of the given poem. It cannot be adequately defined in any other way: there are

no available terms save those which the poem, in its opposing ironies and paradoxes, itself lays down." Jones's imaginative close reading supplies a needed emphasis on the poem's comic dimensions but fails to consider allusions as part of this "complex totality." A valuable reading of the poem appears in Deane Swift's *Essay upon the Life, Writings and Character of Dr Jonathan Swift* (London, 1755), pp. 240–45. Other useful suggestions are added by Martin Price in *Swift's Rhetorical Art* (New Haven: Yale University Press, 1953), pp. 108–9; Ricardo Quintana in *Swift: An Introduction* (London: Oxford University Press, 1955), p. 19; Ronald Paulson in "Swift, Stella, and Permanence," *ELH*, 27 (1960), 312–13; Irvin Ehrenpreis, *Swift*, II, 647–48; and Vivian Mercier, "Swift's Humour," in *Jonathan Swift, 1667–1967: A Dublin Tercentenary Tribute*, ed. Roger McHugh and Philip Edwards (Dublin: The Dolmen Press, 1967), pp. 131–35.

29 Williams, *Poems*, II, 684.

30 Donald R. Roberts, "A Freudian View of Jonathan Swift," *Literature and Psychology*, 6 (1956), 13. The reference is to line 547.

31 Maurice Johnson, *The Sin of Wit: Jonathan Swift as a Poet* (Syracuse, N.Y.: Syracuse University Press, 1950), p. 43.

32 *Ovid's Art of Love* (London, 1709). The quotations of Ovid are from this translation, which went into at least ten editions in the eighteenth century and many more in the nineteenth.

33 Other mock-heroic characteristics in "Cadenus and Vanessa" include the appeal to the muse (ll. 126–27), a heroine (ll. 155–83), the use of "thrice" (ll. 156–59, 177), an epic simile (ll. 51–60), a reference to Fate (l. 485), and the war between the sexes throughout the poem, especially Vanessa's lack of "equal Arms" (l. 621) in the fray. Note also the echoes of *Paradise Lost* in line 155, "*Amaranthine Flow'rs*" (cf. *PL*, XI, 77–78) and in line 487, "Adamantine Chain" (cf. *PL*, I, 48, and elsewhere); of Dryden's *Aeneid* in line 695, "such God-like Men" (cf. II, 1; VII, 59; XI, 19; and XI, 185); and of *The Rape of the Lock* in line 333, "And tell the Murders of her Eyes" (cf. II, 187, of the 1712 version; V, 145, of the 1714 version).

34 *Ovid's Art of Love*, p. 361. Likewise, Chaucer labels her "woful Dido" in *The House of Fame* (l. 318) and in *The Legend of Good Women* calls her "this noble quen Dydo" (l. 1309) and tells how Aeneas "as a traytour forth . . . gan to sayle" and "laft Dido in wo

and pyne" (ll. 1328 and 1330): see *The Works of Geoffrey Chaucer*, ed. F. N. Robinson, 2nd ed. (Boston: Houghton Mifflin, 1957), pp. 285, 503, and 504.

35 *The Poems of John Dryden*, ed. James Kinsley (Oxford: Clarendon Press, 1958), III, 1030–31. The French critics also resisted the pressure toward sentimentalizing: Jean Regnauld de Segrais, *Traduction de l'Enéide de Virgile* (Paris, 1668), pp. 35–40, 92–96; René Le Bossu, *Treatise of the Epick Poem*, trans. W. J. (London, 1695), p. 195; and René Rapin, *Les Oeuvres* (Amsterdam, 1709), I, 144–46.

36 Antony Blackwall, *An Introduction to the Classics*, 6th ed. (London, 1746), p. 192; also p. 229. Barton Booth, at the end of *The Death of Dido: A Masque* (London, 1716), warns damsels, "Lest by Falsehood, or by Fate, / Reduc'd to thy unhappy State, / They trust in Man, and be Undone." By the middle of the century, Joseph Warton could describe Dido as almost a pathetic heroine: "If the reader be not void of all taste and sensibility, pity and humanity, he must be inexpressibly moved, by the following circumstances of Dido's behaviour: by her carrying Aeneas thro' the town, and tempting him to settle in a city already begun to be built; by her beginning to speak and suddenly stopping short and faultering; . . . by her desiring to hear his story again and again; by her attention to every syllable he spoke; by her remaining in the hall after the guests were gone, and lying upon the couch where he sat; by her thinking she still hears his voice, and still sees his person, and by her fondly playing with Ascanius" (*The Works of Virgil, in Latin and English* [London, 1753], II, 276n). Later works show the completion of the movement toward sentimentality: see *Dido, Queen of Carthage; an Opera* ([London], 1792); *Dido, a Tragedy* (London, 1808); and *Dido in Despair* (London, 1821).

37 Swift apparently is echoing Dryden's phrase "an unerring Guide" (*Religio Laici*, l. 227; *The Hind and the Panther*, I, 65; II, 479; II, 683; and III, 423). Phillip Harth has shown that Dryden intended the line in *Religio Laici* as ironic, to deny that such an infallible interpreter exists (*Contexts of Dryden's Thought* [Chicago: University of Chicago Press, 1968], pp. 207–8). I suspect, however, that Swift chose the line for its context, taken literally: "Such an [unerring Guide] we wish indeed" (*Religio Laici*, l. 282).

38 Swift omitted from post-1726 editions a passage that made Vanessa rather flirtatious and forward (*Poems*, II, 704n).

39 *The Poems of John Dryden*, III, 1025.
40 Nahum Tate and Henry Purcell, *Dido and Aeneas* (1689), ed. Edward J. Dent (London: Oxford University Press, 1925), p. 79.
41 *The Works of Virgil: Translated into English Blank Verse. With Large Explanatory Notes, and Critical Observations*, 4th ed. (London, 1755), II, 223.
42 Samuel Johnson, *The Rambler*, No. 121, ed. W. J. Bate and Albrecht B. Strauss, Vol. IV of the Yale Edition of the Works of Samuel Johnson (New Haven: Yale University Press, 1969), p. 284. Cf. Christopher Marlowe, *The Tragedy of Dido, Queen of Carthage*, V, i, 292–94: "Now, Dido, with these relics burn thyself, / And make Aeneas famous through the world / For perjury and slaughter of a queen" (*The Complete Plays of Christopher Marlowe*, ed. Irving Ribner [New York: Odyssey Press, 1963], p. 46).
43 Tyne, "Vanessa and the Houyhnhnms," pp. 526–29 (echoing John Boyle, Earl of Cork and Orrery, *Remarks on the Life and Writings of Dr Jonathan Swift* [London, 1752], pp. 110–12), uses these maxims to attack Vanessa's character as extremist and egotistical. But as Deane Swift pointed out in replying to Orrery, "She availeth herself of the Doctor's own maxims" (*Essay*, p. 246), so Cadenus must take the blame for any moral culpability in them. Deane Swift went on to cite passages from "On seeing Verses written upon Windows in Inns" (1726), ll. 1–8 (*Poems*, II, 400) and "To the Earl of Oxford" (1716), ll. 11–14 (*Poems*, I, 210) as evidence that Swift himself saw at least some merit in these positions (*Essay*, pp. 249–51).
44 See "To Stella, Who Collected and Transcribed his Poems" (1720), ll. 9–14, *Poems*, II, 728. Also see "To Stella, Visiting me in my Sickness" (1720), l. 117, *Poems*, II, 727; "Stella's Birth-Day" (1724/25), ll. 30–32, *Poems*, II, 757; "A Letter to a Young Lady, on her Marriage" (1723), *Prose Works*, IX, 86, 89–90; and Swift to the Rev. James Stopford, 20 July 1726, *Corres.*, III, 145.
45 Leslie Stephen, *Swift* (New York, 1882), p. 127.
46 A. Martin Freeman, ed., *Vanessa and Her Correspondence with Jonathan Swift* (London: Selwyn and Blount, 1921), p. 24.

Chapter IV: The Arts of Love and Friendship

1 "To Stella, Visiting me in my Sickness" (1720), l. 117, *Poems*, II, 727.
2 "A Letter to a Young Lady," *Prose Works*, IX, 89–90.

3 Patrick Delany, *Observations upon Lord Orrery's Remarks on the Life and Writings of Dr. Jonathan Swift* (London, 1754), p. 32, quoted in *Poems*, I, 89.

4 Swift uses, for example, a parallel from classical thought to build a fine tribute to Stella's character and friendship in "To Stella. March 13, 1723–24":

> All accidents of life conspire
> To raise up Stella's virtue higher;
>
> .   .   .   .
>
> Her firmness who could e'er have known,
> Had she not evils of her own?
> (21–22, 25–26)

Seneca notes a like value in affliction: "Prosperity shews a Man but one part of Human Nature. No body knows what such a Man is good for: Neither in truth does he Understand himself, for want of Experiment. . . . He that has liv'd in Popularity and Applause, knows not how he would bear Infamy, and Reproach. . . . Calamity is the Occasion of Virtue, and a Spur to a Great Mind" (Roger L'Estrange, *Seneca's Morals By Way of Abstract*, 11th ed. [London, 1718], pp. 487 and 156). The digression on anger in "To Stella, Who Collected and Transcribed his Poems" uses classical thought in a similar way. As Swift urges calm acceptance "when a Friend in Kindness tries / To shew you where your Error lies" (89–90), Cicero advised that "it is of the Essence of a hearty Friendship, that we should be free in communicating and receiving good Admonitions and Directions; . . . and again, that we should entertain them without Aversion or Impatience" (*Tully's Two Essays of Old Age, and of Friendship. With His Stoical Paradoxes, and Scipio's Dream*, trans. Samuel Parker, 3rd ed. [London, 1727], p. 99). When Stella reacts with anger instead and, "what is worse, your Passion bends / Its Force against your nearest Friends" (97–98), her reaction is just what Plutarch warns against in his essay on anger: we should retreat into a haven when anger attacks, he declares, "lest we fall . . . upon others; and truly we do most, and most frequently fall upon our Friends" (*Plutarch's Morals: Translated from the Greek by Several Hands*, 4th ed. [London, 1704], I, 40).

5 *Tully's Two Essays*, p. 8. John I. Fischer ("The Uses of Virtue: Swift's

Last Poem to Stella," in *Essays in Honor of Esmond Linworth Marilla*, ed. Thomas A. Kirby and William J. Olive [Baton Rouge: Louisiana State University Press, 1970], pp. 201–9) neglects the influence of the classical references when he concludes that the final birthday poem is wholly Christian, a "poetic 'communion of the sick' " with "the single great purpose of Stella's salvation." Fischer's thesis, that "much of the poem is devoted to refuting the opinion, apparently Stella's, that a future state . . . is merely chimerical" (p. 205), takes as an assertive statement about Stella's beliefs what Swift puts hypothetically: "[Even if] future Happiness and Pain, / [were] A mere Contrivance of the Brain" (19–20). Actually Swift excludes Christianity from his consideration of the value of virtue in order to inquire solely from common sense and shared values. The poem emphasizes reason (9, 59, 65) and conducts its discussion in an apparently logical mode, with paragraphs structured about premises and conclusions (9–14, 15–18, 19–34, 55–60, 61–66). Like Pope in *An Essay on Man*, Swift in the final poem to Stella seeks to reinforce Christian positions by reaching them through non-Christian approaches. A valuable study of the Stella poems, though it also overemphasizes their Christian aspects, is James L. Tyne, S.J., "Swift and Stella: The Love Poems," *Tennessee Studies in Literature*, 19 (1974), 35–47.

6 "Stella's Birth-Day" (1724/25), ll. 49–50.

7 Apollodorus, *The Library*, I, iv, 4, trans. Sir James G. Frazer, Loeb Classical Library (London: Heinemann, 1921), I, 33.

8 I am grateful to Felicity Nussbaum for calling this allusion, which is not included in modern editions of the poems, to my attention. Cf. her reading of it in "Juvenal, Swift, and *The Folly of Love*," *Eighteenth-Century Studies*, 9 (1976), 540–52.

9 *Remedia Amoris*, 347–55, *The Art of Love, and Other Poems*, trans. J. H. Mozley, Loeb Classical Library, rev. ed. (London: Heinemann, 1939), p. 203. All translations of the *Remedia Amoris* are from this edition; line numbers and page references for succeeding passages will be included in the text.

10 "Works and Days," 70–82, *The Homeric Hymns and Homerica*, trans. Hugh G. Evelyn-White, Loeb Classical Library, rev. ed. (London: Heinemann, 1936), pp. 7, 9.

11 As, for example, Denis Donoghue, *Jonathan Swift: A Critical Intro-*

duction (Cambridge: Cambridge University Press, 1969), pp. 203–15; Thomas B. Gilmore, Jr., "The Comedy of Swift's Scatological Poems," *PMLA*, 91 (1976), 33–41; E. San Juan, Jr., "The Anti-Poetry of Jonathan Swift," *Philological Quarterly*, 44 (1965), 390–92, 395–96.

12 *Virgil's Aeneis*, I, 780, *The Poems of John Dryden*, ed. James Kinsley (Oxford: Clarendon Press, 1958), III, 1084.

13 From "Venus and Adonis," ll. 962–63, and *Henry V*, II, iii, 54, *The Riverside Shakespeare*, ed. G. Blakemore Evans (Boston: Houghton Mifflin, 1974), pp. 1716, 945.

14 *Aeneid*, IV, 467–68, *Virgil*, trans. H. Rushton Fairclough, Loeb Classical Library, rev. ed. (London: Heinemann, 1932), I, 426–27.

15 John M. Aden, "Corinna and the Sterner Muse of Swift," *English Language Notes*, 4 (1966), 23–31, holds that the juxtaposing of comic and tragic is purposeful and successful. The poem, however, does not move "in alternating scenes of grotesque and pathetic emphasis" (p. 28); rather, the pathetic interjects itself randomly, often at points where it undermines rather than counterbalances the grotesque.

16 John M. Aden, "Those Gaudy Tulips: Swift's 'Unprintables,' " in *Quick Springs of Sense: Studies in the Eighteenth Century*, ed. Larry S. Champion (Athens: University of Georgia Press, 1974), p. 25.

17 R. Ellis Roberts, "Jonathan Swift in His Poems and Minor Writings," in *Reading for Pleasure and Other Essays* (London: Methuen, 1928), p. 213.

18 See also the comments on the poem by A. B. England, "World without Order: Some Thoughts on the Poetry of Swift," *Essays in Criticism*, 16 (1966), 32–36.

19 David M. Vieth, *Notes and Queries*, 220 (1975), 562–63.

20 "Strephon and Chloe," l. 143; "The Progress of Beauty," l. 46; "Verses to Vanessa" (1720), l. 4.

21 Of the scatological poems only "Cassinus and Peter" can be said to be an unqualified success. Its comedy is successful, in part, because it is detached from Swift, almost wholly in dialogue. But the detachment may have been possible because the poem is not really about women or excretion. Successful as it is as a comic exposure of those whose etherealization of women approaches that of Cassinus, one still is led to wonder who, in the eighteenth century, with

its rather unsophisticated facilities for sanitation and bathing, these naïfs were. Even if excrement is used as a symbol, the question of why Swift found this symbol particularly appropriate or effective remains. Katharine M. Rogers, in *The Troublesome Helpmate: A History of Misogyny in Literature* (Seattle: University of Washington Press, 1966), concludes that "the fact that women excrete . . . obviously had an extraordinary emotional impact on him as well as on the lover-protagonists in his poems" (p. 171). See also Bonamy Dobrée, *English Literature in the Early Eighteenth Century, 1700–1740*, Vol. VII of *The Oxford History of English Literature*, ed. F. P. Wilson and Bonamy Dobrée (Oxford: Clarendon Press, 1959), pp. 462–63. To say this is not to invite a return to psychoanalytic criticism: there simply is not enough reliable data to make such an exercise worthwhile. For works that give so much evidence of personal involvement by the author, however, wholly impersonal criticism creates artificial structures and themes which, in the end, lead to misunderstanding of the poems and of the author. For psychoanalytic studies of Swift, see Evelyn Hardy, *The Conjured Spirit: Swift* (London: The Hogarth Press, 1949), pp. 57–59, 176–77; Phyllis Greenacre, *Swift and Carroll: A Psychoanalytic Study of Two Lives* (New York: International Universities Press, 1955), pp. 60–115; and Donald R. Roberts, "A Freudian View of Jonathan Swift," *Literature and Psychology*, 6 (1956), 8–17. For a fine analysis of the weaknesses of such studies, see a review of Greenacre's book by Frederick Wyatt, Deborah Bacon, and Arthur M. Eastman, *Literature and Psychology*, 6 (1956), 18–27.

22 Gilmore, "The Comedy of Swift's Scatological Poems," concludes that "*A Panegyrick on the D——n, in the Person of a Lady in the North* [1730] points a middle way toward an attitude that accepts waste as a natural part of life" (pp. 40–41). To derive this from the poem, however, is to ignore the difference between the Saturnian age in the fable and our own age. In a romanticized, golden world, perhaps it was proper that "The Margin of a purling Stream" oft "Sent up to thee [Cloacine] a grateful Steam" (241–42). In our "degen'rate Days," however, it is more proper to restrain the promptings of nature, to enter the "lofty Domes" (singly, of course: "'tis prophane when Sexes mingle"), and leave one's offering "unobserv'd" (287, 225, 209, 215).

23 E.g., Aldous Huxley, "Swift," in *Do What You Will* (London: Chatto and Windus, 1929), pp. 103–5; Roberts, "Jonathan Swift in His Poems and Minor Writings," pp. 210–13; D. H. Lawrence, *A Propos of Lady Chatterley's Lover* (London: The Mandrake Press, 1930), pp. 13–14; George Orwell, "Politics *vs.* Literature: An Examination of *Gulliver's Travels*," in *Shooting an Elephant and Other Essays* (London: Secker and Warburg, 1950), pp. 81–82; and John Middleton Murry, *Jonathan Swift: A Critical Biography* (London: Jonathan Cape, 1954), pp. 439–42. The redemption of the scatological poems began with Herbert Davis's essay "Swift's View of Poetry," in *Studies in English by Members of University College, Toronto*, collected by Malcolm W. Wallace (Toronto: University of Toronto Press, 1931), esp. pp. 52–56. Other early defenses appeared in the *Johnsonian News Letter*—by Bonamy Dobrée and Maurice Johnson (10, No. 1 [1950], 7–8) and by Clarence L. Kulisheck (10, No. 3 [1950], 11–12)—and in Maurice Johnson's *The Sin of Wit: Jonathan Swift as a Poet* (Syracuse, N.Y.: Syracuse University Press, 1950), pp. 110–21.

24 Johnson, *The Sin of Wit*, pp. 110–21; Herbert Davis, "A Modest Defence of 'The Lady's Dressing Room,' " in *Restoration and Eighteenth-Century Literature: Essays in Honor of Alan Dugald McKillop*, ed. Carroll Camden (Chicago: University of Chicago Press, 1963), pp. 39–48; James L. Tyne, S.J., "Gulliver's Maker and Gullibility," *Criticism*, 7 (1965), 152–58; Donald Greene, "On Swift's 'Scatological' Poems," *Sewanee Review*, 75 (1967), 672–89; Jae Num Lee, *Swift and Scatological Satire* (Albuquerque: University of New Mexico Press, 1971), pp. 82–91.

Chapter V: Neither So Ill a Subject Nor So Stupid an Author

1 *Prose Works*, IX, 25–34 (also printed in *Corres.*, II, 365–74).
2 Swift to Archbishop King, 18 May 1727, *Corres.*, III, 209–11.
3 On death, for example, *Corres.*, III, 354, 375, 382, and 506; the apologetic passages include III, 289, 340–41, 374–75, 396–97, 410–11, 421, 422–23, 434–35, 482–84, and 499–502.
4 See *Corres.*, IV, 116, 335, 382; V, 41.
5 Swift to Pope, 12 May 1735, *Corres.*, IV, 335; also see IV, 547.
6 Swift to Pope, 1 June 1728, *Corres.*, III, 289.
7 Swift to Bolingbroke and Pope, 5 April 1729, *Corres.*, III, 331; Swift

to John Gay, 29 June 1731, *Corres.*, III, 471.

8 "Verses written by Dr. Swift" (1732), *Poems*, II, 611.

9 "The Substance of What was said" (1730), *Prose Works*, XII, 145–48.

10 John Middleton Murry, *Jonathan Swift: A Critical Biography* (London: Jonathan Cape, 1954), p. 457.

11 Swift to Thomas Sheridan, 24 June 1727, *Corres.*, III, 219.

12 See especially a letter to Charles Ford, 18 March 1728/29, *Corres.*, III, 321.

13 Swift to Gay, 19 March 1729/30, *Corres.*, III, 380.

14 Swift to the Earl of Oxford, 28 April 1730, *Corres.*, III, 393.

15 Swift to Gay, 1 December 1731, *Corres.*, III, 506.

16 The personal attacks are often conducted through recurring techniques, particularly through various "*representative Symbols, by Allegories* and *Fables.*" Thus, Walpole is attacked by being compared, over and over, to Cardinal Wolsey and Sejanus; through the "Allegory of the R–ches" and the symbol of a "huge and most sumptuous LANTHORN" in a great palace in Norfolk; and as the hero of "The *Mock Minister; or, Harlequin a Statesman: An Entertainment*, in Characters partly *serious* and partly *grotesque*"—to cite just a few important examples.

17 No. 322, 2 September 1732, in the collected edition, *The Craftsman* (London, 1731–37), IX, 232. Volume and page numbers in subsequent references are from this edition. Swift's knowledge of *The Craftsman* is shown by two allusions to it in "Verses on the Death of Dr. Swift"—line 274 and especially the footnote to line 194: "An excellent Paper, called the *Craftsman.*"

18 *The Occasional Writer* (London, 1727), p. 9. Cf. *The Craftsman*, No. 143, 29 March 1729: "The last Kind of *State Implements*, which I shall mention in this Paper, is That of *Court-Writers*; . . . *Those*, who prostitute their Pens, in a servile Manner, to *make their* Court to *Men in Authority*" (IV, 186). Also see *The Craftsman*, No. 18, 7 February 1726/27 (I, 102).

19 *The Craftsman*, No. 90, 23 March 1727/28 (III, 25, 28).

20 Ibid., No. 209, 4 July 1730 (VI, 223). See also No. 206, 13 June 1730 (VI, 194).

21 Ibid., No. 136, 8 February 1728/29 (IV, 133).

22 Ibid., No. 55, 22 July 1727 (II, 71).

23 Ibid., No. 94, 20 April 1728 (III, 65).

24 James Bramston, *The Art of Politicks* (London, 1729), p. 7. Swift praises Bramston's poem in a letter to Charles Wogan, 2 August 1732, *Corres.*, IV, 54.

25 *Robin's Panegyrick* (London, [1729], 1731, [1733?]). That Swift knew this miscellany is quite possible, since his "Character of Sir Robert Walpole" is printed anonymously as the final item of the third volume; see Peter J. Schakel, " 'The Character of Sir Robert Walpole'; A Previously Unnoticed Publication," *Papers of the Bibliographical Society of America*, 70 (1976), 111–14.

26 William Yonge, *Sedition and Defamation Display'd: In a Letter to the "Craftsman"* (London, 1731), p. i; William Pulteney, *Answer to One Part of a late Infamous Libel* (London, 1731). Similarly, there are repeated references to libel in Bolingbroke's *A Final Answer to the Remarks on the "Craftsman" 's Vindication* (London, 1731).

27 *The Craftsman*, No. 126, 30 November 1728 (IV, 18).

28 Ibid., No. 264, 24 July 1731 (VIII, 62). See also No. 209, 4 July 1730 (VI, 223).

29 Ibid., No. 179, 6 December 1729 (V, 207).

30 Williams, *Corres.*, III, 411n. Cf. Herbert Davis, "Swift's Character," in *Jonathan Swift, 1667–1967: A Dublin Tercentenary Tribute*, ed. Roger McHugh and Philip Edwards (Dublin: The Dolmen Press, 1967), p. 3: "It must be that he claims the privilege to rail, and go unpublished."

31 "The Substance of What was said by the Dean," *Prose Works*, XII, 148.

32 Swift to Pope, 26 February 1729/30, *Corres.*, III, 374.

33 Swift to Pope, 2 May 1730, *Corres.*, III, 396.

34 For the basic critical issues in "Verses on the Death of Dr. Swift," see Barry Slepian, "The Ironic Intention of Swift's Verses on His Own Death," *Review of English Studies*, n.s. 14 (1963), 249–56; Marshall Waingrow, *"Verses on the Death of Dr. Swift," Studies in English Literature*, 5 (1965), 513–18; Arthur H. Scouten and Robert D. Hume, "Pope and Swift: Text and Interpretation of Swift's Verses on His Death," *Philological Quarterly*, 52 (1973), 205–31; and Robert W. Uphaus, "Swift's 'Whole Character': The Delany Poems and 'Verses on the Death of Dr. Swift,' " *Modern Language Quarterly*, 34 (1973), 411–16. David M. Vieth provides a thorough,

convenient review of criticism of the poem in "The Mystery of Personal Identity: Swift's Verses on His Own Death," in *The Author in His Work: Essays on a Problem in Criticism*, ed. Louis L. Martz and Aubrey Williams (New Haven: Yale University Press, 1978), pp. 245–62.

35 "A Letter to the Whole People of Ireland," *Prose Works*, X, 63; see also pp. 67–68.

36 William E. H. Lecky, *A History of Ireland in the Eighteenth Century* (London: Longmans, Green and Co., 1913), I, 241. See also J. T. Ball, *Historical Review of the Legislative Systems Operative in Ireland, from the Invasion of Henry the Second to the Union (1172–1800)* (London, 1888), pp. 13–15, 75–77.

37 E.g., "Near to the *Rose* where Punks in numbers flock / To pick up Cullies, to increase their Stock" (Joseph Addison, "The Play-House," *Poems on Affairs of State: Augustan Satirical Verse, 1660–1714*, Vol. VI, *1697–1704*, ed. Frank H. Ellis [New Haven: Yale University Press, 1970], p. 31). Other such references appear in *The Morning Ramble; or, the Town Humours* (1673); Richard Ames, *The Search after Claret* (1691); Thomas Shadwell, *The Scow'rers* (1691); and *The Rake Reformed* (1718). See also the third plate of William Hogarth, *A Rake's Progress* (1735).

38 *A Tale of a Tub, To which is added The Battle of the Books and the Mechanical Operation of the Spirit*, ed. A. C. Guthkelch and D. Nichol Smith, 2nd ed. (Oxford: Clarendon Press, 1958), p. 221.

39 *The Craftsman*, No. 17, 30 January 1726/27 (I, 101). The dedication to the first volume of the collected edition asserts that "the general Principles of *Liberty* have been the Foundation of all our Arguments" (I, v; see also pp. viii, xx, and xxiv). The political connotations of *liberty* for the Opposition are further revealed by its passing use in *The Craftsman* and by the frequent longer discussions in *The Craftsman* of the nature and preservation of liberty.

40 "To Mr. Delany" (1718), l. 34, *Poems*, I, 216.

41 Charles T. Waller, "Swift's *Apologia Pro Satura Sua*," *Satire News Letter*, 10, No. 1 (1973), 19–25.

42 E.g., Herbert Davis, "Swift's View of Poetry," in *Studies in English by Members of University College, Toronto*, collected by Malcolm W. Wallace (Toronto: University of Toronto Press, 1931), p. 50; Maurice Johnson, *The Sin of Wit: Jonathan Swift as a Poet* (Syracuse,

N.Y.: Syracuse University Press, 1950), pp. 106–7; John M. Bullitt, *Jonathan Swift and the Anatomy of Satire* (Cambridge, Mass.: Harvard University Press, 1953), pp. 34–35.

43 Oliver Goldsmith, *The Beauties of English Poesy* (1767): *Collected Works of Oliver Goldsmith*, ed. Arthur Friedman (Oxford: Clarendon Press, 1966), V, 323; Henry Craik, *The Life of Jonathan Swift* (London, 1882), p. 473. See also Williams, *Poems*, II, 639–40; F. Elrington Ball, *Swift's Verse: An Essay* (London: John Murray, 1929), p. 284; and Ricardo Quintana, *Swift: An Introduction* (London: Oxford University Press, 1955), pp. 180–81.

44 Ricardo Quintana, *The Mind and Art of Jonathan Swift* (London: Oxford University Press, 1936), p. 352. Similarly, Johnson, *The Sin of Wit*, p. 15.

45 I have substituted Faulkner's reading "The Laureat" for "Mr. Fielding," which was, as Faulkner notes, "maliciously inserted" in the London edition (*The Works of Jonathan Swift* [Dublin, 1735], II, 451n).

46 Although other lines follow and the poem was left unfinished, it seems complete, artistically and thematically, at line 480.

47 See James L. Tyne, S.J., "Swift's Mock Panegyrics in 'On Poetry: A Rapsody,' " *Papers on Language and Literature*, 10 (1974), 279–86.

48 *Aeneid*, VI, 769–70. The text and translation are from *Virgil*, trans. H. Rushton Fairclough, Loeb Classical Library (London: Heinemann, 1916), I, 560–61.

49 *Aeneid*, VI, 794–95 (Loeb edition, I, 562–63).

50 Horace, *Epistles*, I, xii, 27–28, *Satires, Epistles and Ars Poetica*, trans. H. Rushton Fairclough, Loeb Classical Library (London: Heinemann, 1926), pp. 330–31.

51 Laurence Eusden, *A Poem Humbly Inscribed To His Royal Highness* (London, 1729), p. 6.

52 Ibid., p. 4.

Chapter VI: With a Prophet's Voice and Power

1 *A Tale of a Tub, To which is added The Battle of the Books and the Mechanical Operation of the Spirit*, ed. A. C. Guthkelch and D. Nichol Smith, 2nd ed. (Oxford: Clarendon Press, 1958), p. 267.

2 Deane Swift, *An Essay upon the Life, Writings and Character of Dr*

Jonathan Swift (London, 1755), p. 198. The allusion is to Deut. 6:7–9 (repeated in 11:19–20).

3 "A Letter to Mr. Harding the Printer" (1724), the Second Drapier's Letter, *Prose Works*, X, 15.

4 *Prose Works*, X, 77; XII, 11–12; X, 24; X, 88; and X, 43.

5 William Kerrigan, *The Prophetic Milton* (Charlottesville: University Press of Virginia, 1974), p. 10.

6 "To Mr. Harding," *Prose Works*, X, 22. The quotation is from Ps. 58:4–5. On the numerous biblical references in the Drapier's Letters, see Charles A. Beaumont, *Swift's Use of the Bible: A Documentation and a Study in Allusion*, University of Georgia Monographs, No. 14 (Athens: University of Georgia Press, 1965), pp. 36–44.

7 "Some Observations Upon a Paper" (1724), the Third Drapier's Letter, *Prose Works*, X, 31.

8 Swift to Alexander Pope, 11 August 1729, *Corres.*, III, 341.

9 Ibid.

10 Swift to Pope, 1 June 1728, *Corres.*, III, 289.

11 Texts and translations are from *Horace: The Odes and Epodes*, trans. C. E. Bennett, Loeb Classical Library (London: Heinemann, 1914).

12 R. P. Sanadon, *Les Poesies D'Horace* (Paris, 1727), I, 258. Also see André Dacier, *Les Oeuvres D'Horace*, 2nd ed. (Paris, 1691), I, 196–97.

13 Prov. 21:3; similarly, 1 Sam. 15:22; Hos. 6:6; Matt. 9:13.

14 "An Answer to a Paper, Called *A Memorial*" (1728), *Prose Works*, XII, 22–23. The quotation is from Prov. 1:20–26.

15 Matt. 13:15, quoted in "To Mr. Harding," *Prose Works*, X, 22.

16 Cf. "It is certain, that a firm *Union* in any Country, where every Man wishes the same Thing with relation to the Publick, may, in several Points of the greatest Importance, in some Measure, supply the *Defect of Power*; and even of *those Rights which are the natural and undoubted Inheritance of Mankind*" ("An Humble Address to both Houses of Parliament" [1725], *Prose Works*, X, 134).

17 "A Letter to the Whole People of Ireland" (1724), the Fourth Drapier's Letter, *Prose Works*, X, 63.

18 "An Humble Address," *Prose Works*, X, 126–27.

19 "A Proposal that All the Ladies and Women of Ireland should appear constantly in Irish Manufactures" (1729), *Prose Works*, XII, 126.

20 "A Modest Proposal" (1729), *Prose Works*, XII, 117.

21 Besides the allusion to Mark 5:9, which these lines share with "The Legion Club," the lines echo Rev. 12:10 and John 8:41–44.

22 Patrick Delany thought it "far excels every other of his poetic performances" (*Observations* [London, 1754], p. 118). Also see John Churton Collins, *Jonathan Swift: A Biographical and Critical Study* (London, 1893), pp. 225–27; Maurice Johnson, *The Sin of Wit: Jonathan Swift as a Poet* (Syracuse, N.Y.: Syracuse University Press, 1950), pp. 100–105; John Middleton Murry, *Jonathan Swift: A Critical Biography* (London: Jonathan Cape, 1954), pp. 471–74; and Denis Donoghue, *Jonathan Swift: A Critical Introduction* (Cambridge: Cambridge University Press, 1969), pp. 215–17.

23 The biblical commentators illustrate the appropriateness of applying this passage to the Irish Parliament. Matthew Poole, for example, comments as follows on Mark 5:1–20: "We have also shewed [the Devil's] Power, which (by God's permission) he exerciseth upon Men, some he *possesseth*, and acteth the part of the Soul in them . . . these are properly called *Demoniacks*" (*Annotations Upon the Holy Bible* [London, 1683–85], Vol. II; this translates, rather freely, the *Synopsis Criticorum* [London, 1669–76], which Swift owned [Harold Williams, *Dean Swift's Library* (Cambridge: Cambridge University Press, 1932), p. 3]). Similarly, Lapide: "Wherefore if any one determines to serve God perfectly [e.g., the Irish Clergy?], let him be well assured that he has arrayed against him, not one legion of devils only, but many, even Satan himself, and all the dwellers in hell" (*The Great Commentary of Cornelius à Lapide*, Vol. IV of *The Gospels*, trans. Thomas W. Mossman, 4th ed. [Edinburgh: John Grant, 1908], p. 224, a literal translation of the well-known Latin original [Lyons, 1638]).

24 Joseph Horrell, ed., *Collected Poems of Jonathan Swift* (London: Routledge and Kegan Paul, 1958), II, 803. Similarly, William George Smith, *The Oxford Dictionary of English Proverbs* (Oxford: Clarendon Press, 1935), p. 454, and Morris Palmer Tilley, *A Dictionary of the Proverbs in England in the Sixteenth and Seventeenth Centuries* (Ann Arbor: University of Michigan Press, 1950), p. 101.

25 See D. A. Chart, "The Close Alliance of Church and State, 1702–1760," in *History of the Church of Ireland*, ed. Walter Alison Phillips, III (London: Oxford University Press, 1933), 218–19. I shall take

"club" to refer to the entire Parliament (as it does in *Corres.*, IV, 397, 449, 487, and 556), although only the Commons acted on the agistment matter. The Lords, however, had already proven their right to membership: see *Poems*, III, 801–5; also, *Prose Works*, XII, xxxvi–ix and 179–202.

26 "I have been taught, and do believe [it] to be, in some Manner, the *Voice* of God" ("An Humble Address," *Prose Works*, X, 127).

27 "Now tho we read of no other things sold there, but what were useful for Sacrifices, yet this was a Civil use, and a Profanation of that *Holy Place*" (Poole, *Annotations*, on Matt. 21:12–13).

28 "An Epistle to a Lady" is his only other major poem in trochaics (*Poems*, II, 628–38); see also *Poems*, II, 522–23, 572–74, 660–61; III, 799–801, 906–8, 930, 933. The alternation between seven- and eight-syllable lines appears in several of these, but without apparent regularity or purpose.

29 Compare the stable focus of Hogarth's early conversation pieces (the eye goes out and back, not around) with the circular movement created by *The Lottery* (1721); *A Harlot's Progress* (1732), esp. plates 3 and 5; and almost any plate of *A Rake's Progress* (1735). In works later than "The Legion Club," Hogarth achieves a similar effect by the use of straight lines in *Beer Street* (1750–51) and for the Industrious 'Prentice (*Industry and Idleness*, 1747), and of circular ones in *Gin Lane* and for the Idle 'Prentice. Cf. Ronald Paulson, comp., *Hogarth's Graphic Works* (New Haven: Yale University Press, 1965), I, 47.

30 Texts and translations are from *Virgil*, trans. H. Rushton Fairclough, Loeb Classical Library, rev. ed. (London: Heinemann, 1932).

31 Servius: "This is the first: just as she begot the Titans against Saturn, she afterward begot the giants against Jove: and stories were, from anger against the gods Terra created the Titans in her vengeance" (Virgil, *Opera*, ed. Georgius Fabricius [Basil, (1586)], col. 1077; my translation). I am not asserting that Swift knew, or was influenced by, these words, or even this particular commentator. But the traditions shared by most of the commentators were familiar to all educated men at the time.

32 Badius: "He thought they were the first of those who by rash enterprise tried to drive out the gods" (Virgil, *Opera*, ed. Jodocus Badius

Ascensius [Paris, (1507)], fol. 366ʳ; my translation). Dryden's free translation of the passage confirms the point: "The Rivals of the Gods, the *Titan* Race" (VI, 782).

33 See the biography by Charles Harding Firth in the *DNB*.

34 Pontanus: "These, putting mountains on mountains, tried to ascend to heaven, and to push Jove down. In the underworld they arę bound fast back to back by serpents to a column. Hyginus, 28" (*Symbolarum Libri XVII P. Virgilii Maronis Bucolica, Georgica, Aeneis*, ed. Jacobus Pontanus [Lyons, 1604], cols. 1471-72; my translation).

35 See Tiberius Donatus, in Virgil, *Opera*, ed. Fabricius, col. 1076. Also see *Poems*, I, 352-53.

36 Servius, in Virgil, *Opera*, ed. Fabricius, cols. 1077-78; my translation.

37 See Pontanus, col. 1477.

38 Cerda, in Virgil, *Opera Omnia*, ed. Joanne Ludovico de la Cerda (Cologne, 1642-47), I, 689; my translation.

39 The quotations, in my translations, are from Pontanus, col. 1471; Pontanus, col. 1473; and Donatus in Virgil, *Opera*, ed. Badius, fol. 367ᵛ.

40 Joseph Spence, *Polymetis* (London, 1747), p. 259.

Conclusion

1 July–2 August 1732, *Corres.*, IV, 52.

2 Bonamy Dobrée, *English Literature in the Early Eighteenth Century, 1700-1740*, Vol. VII of *The Oxford History of English Literature*, ed. F. P. Wilson and Bonamy Dobrée (Oxford: Clarendon Press, 1959), p. 468; Oliver Ferguson, *Jonathan Swift and Ireland* (Urbana: University of Illinois Press, 1962), p. 182; John Middleton Murry, *Jonathan Swift: A Critical Biography* (London: Jonathan Cape, 1954), p. 471.

3 Maurice Johnson, *The Sin of Wit: Jonathan Swift as a Poet* (Syracuse, N.Y.: Syracuse University Press, 1950), p. 100.

Index

For the reader's convenience, all titles are put in italics, whether or not italicized in the text.

PROSE WORKS

JACKET DESIGNED BY TED SMITH/GRAPHICS
COMPOSED BY FOCUS/TYPOGRAPHERS, ST. LOUIS, MISSOURI
MANUFACTURED BY McNAUGHTON & GUNN, ANN ARBOR, MICHIGAN
TEXT AND DISPLAY LINES ARE SET IN GOUDY

ŨŨ

Library of Congress Cataloging in Publication Data
Schakel, Peter J
The poetry of Jonathan Swift.
Includes bibliographical references and index.
1. Swift, Jonathan, 1667-1745—Poetic works.
2. Swift, Jonathan, 1667-1745—Style.
3. Allusions in literature.
I. Swift, Jonathan, 1667-1745.
II. Title.
PR3728.P58S3   821'.5   78-53292
ISBN 0-299-07650-4